What people are

Spiritual Revelations fr...

At a time of increasing mainstream acceptance of the near-death and other extraordinary experiences, this book gifts poetic insight to many of the core themes that make such experiences so exceptional. Importantly, it does so through the direct voices of the experiencers. As many ancient wisdom paths teach, it is not the spiritual experience itself that matters most, but rather, what one does with the wisdom gained. The revelations you will find within may bring solace to those wondering if there really is "More" than the mundane world, and what (if anything) might happen beyond this physical life. But more significantly, when the insights within are truly integrated and lived in one's day-to-day life, we can immediately end much needless suffering on this planet and begin to truly embody more of our collective human potential. And THAT is most exciting!
–**Dr. Nicole Gruel**, PhD in Transpersonal Psychology, Life Coach to Experiencers of the Extraordinary, Lead Facilitator of IANDS Sharing Groups Online

I highly recommend this exhaustive and clear book which has the great quality of presenting the subject in an objective way by avoiding the bias of any specific religion; a fault that is sadly too often found in much of this literature. The format, based on presenting a large selection of well-chosen testimonials directly from the first-hand accounts of NDErs, further contributes to its impartiality and objectivity. The book's structure is suitable for a variety of readers, from the "novices" in the field to those who already have previous readings, or have had personal experiences and need to find external validation to accept their own. It will provide help and support to those who fear death, are terminally ill, or are suffering from the loss of a dear one.

–**Dr. Renata Bartoli**, Philologist, NDEr, Hypnotherapist and Coordinator of the London, UK IANDS Peer Group

As a practicing psychologist, I found Professor Hodgson's book an insightful and incisive "deep dive" into the nature of NDEs ("near-death experiences"). Leveraging from the NDE evidence base of IANDS, the author has collated and summarized magnificently the key elements of NDEs, amplifying further the phenomena of NDEs and the moral/ethical implications that NDEs hold for humanity. This book is a valuable addition to the reference shelf of both laypersons and investigators for their life-after-death research.

–**Dr. Terry Olesen**, Committee Member and Contributor Researcher, The Australian Institute of Parapsychological Research; Writer/Researcher at Reincarnation Research Limited, USA

This book is a great comfort companion for those living! Reading the experiencers' accounts seeds an expansion of one's mind and heart, inspiring a more meaningful way of living that goes beyond the physical and into the infinity of the soul. Set out in common themed categories with the author's commentary, the reader is assisted in enjoying the reflection and insight into the mysterious phenomena of Near-Death Experiences.

–**Joyce Bok**, Psychologist and Vice President, Australian Institute of Parapsychological Research (AIPR)

Douglas Hodgson has brought light, knowledge and wisdom where there can be uncertainty in relation to the spirit world. Reading this book will help you to expand your spirit and your light and reactivate a memory deep within you. The many stories that are shared allow the reader to glimpse our true home in the Light.

– **Shawn Leonard**, Indigenous Psychic Medium and presenter of the television series *Spirit Talker*

It can be a lonely path for many who experience NDE, bereavement or the fear of death. I found this book to be a great comfort in these cases, and a fascinating exploration of the journey of the soul. There is a great amount of documented NDE cases. What I like about this book is the way it covers, organizes and breaks down the common principles found in the hundreds of near-death experiences, leading the reader to a positive and empowering conclusion. I recommend this work by Professor Douglas Hodgson both for the knowledge it imparts and for the light it shines on the meaning of life.

– **Rachel Langford**, MSc. Med, MBPsS, Neuroscientist, researcher and clinician; a researcher at the NDE support group in the United Kingdom

Spiritual Revelations from Beyond the Veil

What Humanity Can Learn from the
Near-Death Experience

Other Books Written by this Author

The Human Right to Education
(Dartmouth, Aldershot, Hampshire, England, 1998)
ISBN: 1-85521-909-3

Individual Duty within a Human Rights Discourse
(Ashgate, Aldershot, Hampshire, England, 2003)
ISBN: 0-7546-2361-0

The Law of Intervening Causation
(Ashgate, Aldershot, Hampshire, England, 2008)
ISBN: 978-0-7546-7366-8

International Human Rights and Justice
(Nova Science Publishers, Inc., New York, NY, USA, 2016)
(Editor)
ISBN: 978-1-63484-709-4

Transcendental Spirituality, Wisdom and Virtue: The Divine Virtues and Treasures of the Heart
(John Hunt Publishing, Winchester, Hampshire, England, 2023)
ISBN: 978-1-80341-143-9

Spiritual Revelations from Beyond the Veil

What Humanity Can Learn from the Near-Death Experience

Douglas Charles Hodgson

BOOKS

Winchester, UK
Washington, USA

JOHN HUNT PUBLISHING

First published by O-Books, 2023
O-Books is an imprint of John Hunt Publishing Ltd., 3 East St., Alresford,
Hampshire SO24 9EE, UK
office@jhpbooks.com
www.johnhuntpublishing.com
www.o-books.com

For distributor details and how to order please visit the 'Ordering' section on our website.

ISBN: 978 1 80341 340 2
978 1 80341 341 9 (ebook)
Library of Congress Control Number: 2022943436

A CIP catalogue record for this book is available from the British Library.

Design: Lapiz Digital Services

UK: Printed and bound by CPI Group (UK) Ltd, Croydon, CR0 4YY
Printed in North America by CPI GPS partners

The author of this book does not dispense medical advice or
prescribe the use of any technique as a form of treatment for
physical, emotional, or medical problems without the advice of a
physician, either directly or indirectly. The intent of the author
is only to offer information of a general nature to help you in
your quest for emotional and spiritual well-being. In the event
you use any of the information in this book for yourself, which is
your constitutional right, the author and the publisher assume no
responsibility for your actions.

We operate a distinctive and ethical publishing philosophy in
all areas of our business, from our global network of authors to
production and worldwide distribution.

Contents

Preface   1

Chapter 1   Introduction   5

Chapter 2   God/The Source   11

Chapter 3   A Glimpse of Heaven   15

Chapter 4   Interconnectedness/Oneness   23

Chapter 5   The Nature of the Soul-Consciousness   28

Chapter 6   Liberation of the Soul-Consciousness   32

Chapter 7   Higher Spiritual Realms   37

Chapter 8   Universal Metaphysical Knowledge and
            Understanding   51

Chapter 9   Communication in the Spiritual Realms   56

Chapter 10 Our Earthly Life's Purpose and Meaning   59

Chapter 11 Soul Agreements   67

Chapter 12 The Gift of Free Will   70

Chapter 13 Loving Yourself   74

Chapter 14 Living Fully in the Present Moment   76

Chapter 15 Loving Nature and All Life-Forms   78

Chapter 16 The Universal Laws of Attraction and
            Cause and Effect (Karma)   82

Chapter 17 Positive and Negative Energy   85

Chapter 18 Our Physical Body, Its Limitations and
            Eventual Demise   97

Chapter 19 Our Spiritual Re-Birth and Life-Review   104

Chapter 20 Potpourri   116

Chapter 21 Conclusion   122

Author Biography   133

Sources/Recommended Reading   135

Consciousness precedes Being and not the other way around. For this reason, the salvation of this human world lies nowhere else than within the human heart, in the human power to reflect, in human modesty, and in human responsibility. Without a global revolution in the sphere of human consciousness, nothing will change for the better.
– Václav Havel

A human being is part of the whole called by us universe, a part limited in time and space. We experience ourselves, our thoughts and feelings as something separate from the rest. A kind of optical delusion of consciousness. The delusion is a kind of prison for us, restricting us to our personal desires and to affection for a few persons nearest to us. Our task must be to free ourselves from the prison by widening our circle of compassion to embrace all living creatures and the whole of nature in its beauty. The true value of a human being is determined by the measure and the sense in which they have obtained liberation from the self. We shall require a substantially new manner of thinking if humanity is to survive.
– Albert Einstein

Preface

Many of us consider only fleetingly, and seldom profoundly, certain of life's larger questions. Does God exist? What happens when I die? Is there an afterlife? Does Heaven exist? What other spiritual realms and dimensions exist? Do I possess a soul or consciousness that survives the death of my physical body? What is the purpose of my Earthly existence and what is my place in the Universe? Am I judged on a reward-punishment basis and are fear and judgment part of the higher spiritual realms? Is karma real and, if so, how does it operate? Do universal laws exist which underpin the Universe and all of Creation?

In a recently published book entitled *Transcendental Spirituality, Wisdom and Virtue: The Divine Virtues and Treasures of the Heart,* I identified 36 Divine Virtues which form the spiritual and ethical foundations common to all of the world's great religions and belief systems. The purposes of writing this book were to assist readers to identify with and elevate their own spirituality, to better understand their own religion or faith through a spiritual prism and to encourage them to understand and appreciate the spiritual and ethical unity of these religions. Throughout this book, spirituality was very much anchored within a religious context. The sacred scriptures of these religions divulged a wealth of insights into God and God's attributes, Divine knowledge and understanding, the meaning and purpose of life on Earth and various moral and ethical tenets we should aspire to in order to live a better and more wholesome life.

Upon completion of this book, my attention turned to examining the intriguing accounts of various people who had undergone a so-called "near-death experience" and had written about their experiences and what they had learned while they were outside of their physical body. A treasure trove of material

1

was located on the website of the International Association for Near-Death Studies (IANDS) containing hundreds of accounts written by such people. What they described in their written accounts included but went well beyond what can be found in the sacred scriptures. These accounts contained vivid descriptions of Heaven and the higher spiritual realms, what interconnectedness/oneness means, the nature and liberation of the soul-consciousness, the gift of Free Will and its purpose, the nature of soul agreements, the Universal Laws of Attraction and Cause and Effect, the nature of positive and negative energy, the significance of the death of our physical body and our post-physical death spiritual re-birth and life-review. The study and collation of these accounts and the identification of common observations and insights drawn therefrom culminated in the writing of *Spiritual Revelations from Beyond the Veil: What Humanity Can Learn from the Near-Death Experience*. Unlike my first book, this book decouples spirituality from a religious context. Indeed, numerous IANDS authors declared that before their near-death experience, they had no religion and did not believe in the existence of God or an afterlife, while others who were adherents to a particular religion or faith declared that after their experience, their particular religion was of less importance to them and henceforth aspired to be more spiritual in their outlook on life and in their dealings with others and the natural environment.

For those who are terminally ill or who fear the death of their physical body (or indeed life itself), for those who are grieving the loss of a loved one and for those who feel lost and confused about the meaning and purpose to their lives and what lies ahead of them, it is hoped that this book will provide comfort, peace, solace, assurance and direction. The messages from beyond the veil presented in this book are clear, compelling, easy to understand and life-changing. They will dispel various illusions and delusions which burden our spirit and prevent us from progressing our soul's evolutionary journey.

Douglas Hodgson

Chapter 1

Introduction

What happens when we die? Is there an afterlife? And what form and description might that take? Does God exist? And is there a Heaven (or Heavens)? Do each of us have a soul or consciousness that survives the death of our physical body? Do each of us have a unique and tailored mission on Earth and what is the purpose or rationale to our existence here? Are we judged on a reward-punishment basis or are we assisted in a process of spiritual development through reflection by higher beings from other realms? These are all fundamental metaphysical questions in the sense that they cannot be answered through objective study of material reality; they are largely beyond human sense perception and experience. Nevertheless, virtually all of us have a vested interest in the answers to at least some of these questions, although being caught up in the daily distractions and attractions of this world may draw us away from pondering these questions to the extent that perhaps we should.

For the past three centuries or so, scientific materialism and reductionism have postulated that only physical matter exists and that a separate consciousness cannot subsist outside the human body; consciousness exclusively depends upon the functioning of the human brain and the body's physiology. This view has been widely and conventionally held and shared by the scientific and medical communities. This consensus, however, is now being challenged and there is an emerging recognition within the medical research and scientific communities (including in the subatomic quantum physics field) that the human soul or consciousness survives the death of the physical body. The human brain does not create consciousness but is a mere filter of it, and that such consciousness is eternal by nature.

The so-called phenomenon of near-death experience reveals that the soul or consciousness survives the death of the physical body. Although accounts of such experiences date back to antiquity, they have only been systematically collected, documented and researched over the past 50 years or so by such notable researchers as doctors Raymond Moody Jr., PhD, MD and Elisabeth Kübler-Ross, MD. Interest in this topic was reignited almost a decade ago when Eben Alexander, MD and neurosurgeon, published an account of his own near-death experience in *Proof of Heaven: A Neurosurgeon's Journey into the Afterlife*. Hundreds of accounts or narratives of near-death experiences written by those who experienced them are to be found on the website of the International Association for Near-Death Studies, Inc. (IANDS).

Near-death experiences have had a deeply profound and life-changing effect upon those who have experienced them. They involve persons who were resuscitated after having been pronounced clinically dead by medically qualified staff or who came very close to death without being pronounced clinically dead. The near-death experience has particularly impacted on those who have experienced them in relation to how we are supposed to live our lives and what our purpose or mission is in the Earthly plane. They have also significantly altered their views on death and the afterlife.

What then may a near-death experience (NDE) typically involve? While no two such experiences are identical, most share at least a number of common features which appear in the written accounts. Those who experience an NDE report a feeling of suddenly being outside of their physical body in what has been described by some as a black velvety void. They perceive their own body below them as a neutral and emotionally detached observer. They experience peace and a warmth in this void and eventually perceive a pinprick of bright white light far off in the distance. Suddenly their soul begins to drift towards this light through a long dark tunnel or deep valley, eventually gaining great speed as the light appears ever closer. Then upon reaching the threshold of this intense brilliant golden white light, other spiritual beings arrive to greet them, often consisting of deceased relatives and friends. Music filled with majesty and beauty is often heard. They are then joined by a Being of Light of indescribably kind, gentle and loving energy which assists the experiencer with what might be called a "life-review" in which are instantaneously displayed through visual imagery significant events in their lifetime. A nonverbal, almost telepathic communication then takes place which is designed to assist the experiencer in reflecting upon and assessing that lifetime and how they might have been more selfless and less selfish in acting or failing to act in relation to those events. A barrier or veil then appears – often in the form of a fence, door or body of water like a stream or pond – demarcating a boundary or limit between the Earthly plane and the afterlife and the higher spiritual realms of existence. But before crossing over, the experiencer is advised that they must return to their physical body as it is not yet their time. They still must complete their life mission and/or other responsibilities of a familial nature. The decision to return is often a very difficult one, as the experiencer is now used to experiencing sublime and unearthly love, peace, contentment and bliss. Nevertheless the experiencer must return and does so, afterwards recalling varying degrees of the experience and what was communicated. Most experiencers report that this is a profound life-changing experience, particularly in relation to them no longer fearing death and clarity concerning what our true role or mission is in our Earthly life. Some also report that they eventually become less religious and more spiritual. Many state that what they experienced was far different than a dream or hallucination and was more real than anything they have experienced in their Earthly life, being able to recall vividly and accurately what happened to them many years later.

Some of the messages or revelations brought back from the near-death experience are deceptively and disarmingly simple to comprehend while other concepts appear beyond human comprehension and perhaps even beyond plausibility. Many of those who have undergone a near-death experience use the term "ineffable" (inexpressible in words) or indescribable to explain their out-of-body experience and what they encountered. As one IANDS author has described, "It is not possible to convey the richness of my near-death experience with words; it is a bit like trying to depict a magnificent sunset by drawing it in sand with a stick." This is due in part to the fact that human language and linguistics are just too impoverished to accurately and meaningfully describe the true nature of the afterlife or the so-called Ultimate Reality. Furthermore, their frame of reference is confined to their Earthbound experience and perceptive capabilities, and much of what they experienced in the other realms has no Earthly counterpart.

The book's methodological approach is as follows. Some 500 accounts or narratives, written by those who have undergone a near-death experience, which have been collated and displayed on the IANDS website, have been analyzed, with the focus being to identify common observations and themes which appear to emerge from these reports. These observations have then been grouped together in a separate book chapter to reflect a particular theme or topic. The accounts were all anonymously written and no identifying information has been included. Each dot point represents a separate account or narrative observation. As the reader will note, numerous observations and perceptions, while taken from separate accounts, are strikingly similar and tend to corroborate one another. Those observations and perceptions which were consistently repeated across the accounts and remarkably similar to each other form the bulk of the material presented in this book. On relatively few occasions, some "one-off" observations are noted due to their unique and interesting nature. While every effort has been made to preserve the integrity and accuracy of each observation as it appeared in the IANDS account, it has sometimes been necessary to slightly paraphrase the wording to remedy issues of expression and/or grammar.

What then is the purpose of this book? It is to provide comfort and assurance to those who have fear or uncertainty about the eventual demise of their physical bodies. It is to reassure them that their souls are eternal and that there is a beautiful afterlife to be enjoyed within the higher spiritual realms (our true Home). It is to reveal that there is so much more to existence and reality than this life on Earth and our physical body. It is to reveal our purpose for being on Earth, one which is remarkably simple to comprehend although sometimes difficult to achieve in practice. It is to reveal in a preliminary way observations and revelations on God the Source and Creator and Heaven, the interconnectedness of everything, and on universal metaphysical knowledge and understanding including various types of positive and negative energy. It is to provide validation and corroboration to those who have had a near-death experience in relation to what they observed and learned while outside their body. And finally it is to describe how our soul is an eternal work-in-progress, evolving continuously towards communion with the Light/Source.

What you are about to read you may well find remarkable in some respects, indeed even beyond Earthly/human comprehension. Some of you may be receptive to the spiritual revelations which the experiencers have brought back with them while others may be summarily dismissive of what they read. We each have Free Will to do so. What I ask of readers is to try to retain an open and expansive mind when reading this book, as what the experiencers experienced while outside of their physical bodies has invariably brought about a dramatic and lasting life-changing difference to those who returned from the veil to tell their story. The spiritual revelations they returned with may well have a significant influence on us in terms of how we formulate our views on "death" and on how we live our lives henceforward, in alignment with the Divine purpose to continuously and eternally learn and evolve our souls.

Chapter 2

God/The Source

Numerous IANDS accounts refer to experiencing the presence of God or some similar description such as the Light, Love, the Source, Oneness or the Universal Consciousness. It is described as being eternal, infinite, incorporeal, all-knowing, the Creator of All That Is and the Bestower of all life and being. It is energy which permeates all things. The reports observe that there are many religious and spiritual pathways to God.

Nevertheless, the Holy Scriptures of the mainstream religions caution that God cannot be fully comprehended or described in finite human terms or words. Once again, our human language and limiting and restrictive Earthbound experience are such that it is impossible to do justice to expressing the essence or true nature of God. These sentiments are often expressed by the authors of the IANDS accounts but they do try to encapsulate in words what they experienced and learned with this significant caveat attached. The following is what various authors have described concerning their encounters with God and God's supra-human qualities and attributes as well as any messages or revelations which were imparted to them either by God or higher spiritual beings.

- God exists as well as an afterlife beyond our earthly life.
- My near-death experience has left me with a profound certainty that God exists.
- God is the center and we are all spokes of the universal wheel.
- God is our Creator and our soul returns to Him.
- God is an entity of infinite loving energy without beginning or end; subsisting in every dimension, seen and unseen.

- God is never-ending infinity and love, contained in each and every thing.
- God is a spiritual unity, a oneness, universal intelligence existing in the spiritual fourth dimension.
- God is all of the dark energy and dark matter in the whole of the void.
- God created us and dwells within us. To God we are all important and beautiful.
- God is within each of us and speaks to us within.
- God and eternity are within you.
- God resides within us; within our heart, soul and spirit.
- God is immanent within His creation but the creation is all a part of God.
- We are not God, but God is us.
- Peacefully surrender to God and your pain and anxiety will dissipate.
- Give yourself completely and consciously to the Almighty.
- We are never separated from God.
- We are never alone.
- The Universe was created out of love and we are all part of that Creation.
- God is present within every energy particle of the Universe which is without beginning or end.
- We are all unconditionally loved by God.
- God loves us all so very much as we are all His children.
- God is unconditional love beyond human words.
- God loves and cherishes as priceless each of us as we are; we must do the same towards others.
- God loves us just the way we are.
- Behold God in Nature and other people.
- God loves us beyond measure and wants us to trust Him with our earthly journey.
- We are all loved and cherished and never judged by the Creator.

- God is the Light and Energy permeating all of Creation and imbuing everything with being.
- Everyone and everything is God.
- God is the energy of love that binds everything together and underpins all of the laws of physics.
- The Light of God is peace, bliss, comfort, wisdom, joy, compassion and authority.
- The Light of God is absolute unconditional, ineffable love, acceptance and forgiveness.
- The Light is all-knowingness and a peace that surpasses all human understanding.
- God is Light and we are all children of the Light. We are truly never alone.
- God is all-knowledge/omniscience.
- God knows everything about us and every thought that we have ever had. He knows our essence better than we know ourselves.
- The Light is the manifestation of God's presence when He breathes.
- I understood that the intense glowing light was the presence of God.
- The Light is the heart of God.
- Stand in the light of the heart of God.
- God = L.O.V.E. (Light, Oneness, Vibrations and Energy).
- All of us are children of God and loved by Our Creator beyond measure.
- God appeared before me. The Divine Supreme Intelligence. The Light that surrounded Him, that enveloped Him, that was Him, was almost blinding. He is Love. I felt it. I knew it. I knew Him. I was part of Him.
- Pray to the God of your heart rather than the one you have been taught by others. God does not condemn or punish but loves His creatures as they are, and helps them to become better versions of themselves.

- Love and praise God.
- Seek the Creator of all Creation Who created you to find Him. Desire to know your Creator and all things will be added unto you.
- God is everything and manifests in all energy.
- God is the energy of Love.
- The white energy of God fills us to overflowing.
- Race, religion and countries separate humans. God unites.
- God's assurances are threefold: You are unconditionally loved beyond measure. Everything is always as it is supposed to be in the soul's journey. Everything will always be all right.
- Everything is always as it is supposed to be. Everything will always be alright.
- God told me that everything is all right and unfolding as it should.
- Connect to All That Is.
- Connect with Source energy.
- There is no single right way to worship God.
- There is no one true religion or pathway to Heaven. Whatever speaks to our hearts individually is the best path for us. All paths lead us to the Source.
- Cultivate a strong spiritual faith in God, the Source and the Highest Power.
- Have a spiritual, rather than a religious, faith in God.
- God's realm is a timeless, expansive and peaceful void.
- God has no form or embodiment. What could contain the Eternal?
- Universal Consciousness – love, kindness and joy – is the ultimate reality; physical matter and the material world are insubstantial by comparison. Our souls have always been embedded within and cradled by it.

Chapter 3

A Glimpse of Heaven

Most of us have pondered at some point in our lives what Heaven must be like or, indeed, whether Heaven exists at all beyond the realm of mythology. Such a place or concept is mentioned in the Holy Scriptures of most of the mainstream religions but by and large is not described in any concrete or graphic detail. Some religions like Islam and Jainism refer to multiple or ascending heavens. This is indeed supported by at least one of the near-death experience reports.

Many, but not all, of those who have experienced a near-death experience do report that they found themselves in Heaven or at least at the threshold or boundary of Heaven from where they could get a close glimpse of what lay beyond the veil, the fence, the door, the stream, the pond or other forms of barrier between Earthly life and Heaven. The individual descriptions of what they perceived do corroborate each other in many respects as will become apparent in the following observations taken directly from the IANDS near-death experience accounts.

Once again, those who report such experiences state their frustration at not being able to fully, accurately and meaningfully describe what they perceived due to human language barriers and limiting Earthbound experience. However, their descriptive attempts are multidimensional: Heaven can be considered a state of mind, an emotional experience (including joy, bliss and euphoria), a spiritual frame of reference in which negative energy or anything not of the Love or Light is not permitted to enter, or a physical description by the soul's sense perception capacities (mostly vision and sound but not as these senses are experienced on Earth). Many authors of near-death accounts note the radiantly beautiful unearthly colors of Heaven which appear to be alive and pulsating. The descriptions of Heaven are also circumscribed by the Divine attributes of unconditional love, acceptance, knowledge and understanding, peace, forgiveness and truth. Numerous accounts detail an intensely brilliant golden white Light which appears to have life and identity of its own. Many individual IANDS accounts refer to Heaven as our real home.

The following observations on Heaven are taken from the individual IANDS reports studied.

- I was walking and talking with two spiritual beings and we approached a line or horizon with a glorious Light emanating from beyond. They turned to me and told me that I had to go back and that it was not my time (as I had more to accomplish in my Earthly life). I adamantly refused to return but it was to no avail and I instantaneously found myself back in my body.

- The next thing I knew I was in a beautiful garden. I saw a female figure dressed in a long white robe. We were standing near a flower-covered arch. Everything was very peaceful. The woman told me that I was not allowed to pass through the arch because if I did I would not be able to return (to my earthly life).

- I entered a brilliant white light which was extremely bright but not hard on the eyes. I soon sensed that I was not alone. I then saw what I can best describe as an opaque window or screen like a shower curtain. I saw silhouettes of sorts and sensed that I knew these beings. I wanted to go to them but was told that it was not my time.

- There is just not one Heaven; there are many levels to Heaven.

- Heaven is complete and unconditional acceptance and understanding where fear, anger, resentment and self-blame have no place.

- Heaven is indescribable peace and total pure and unconditional love, acceptance and understanding of everything. Pain, fear and shame are unknown there. Heaven is love beyond comprehension.
- Anger, hatred, aggression and fear are never permitted to enter Heaven.
- Heaven is peace and bliss that surpass all human understanding.
- I felt at home before the Light.
- Heaven is our real home. It is joy, contentment, comfort, warmth and love.
- Heaven is rapturous joy and love.
- Heaven is a sense of euphoria, perfect peace and of being home. No pain, wants or needs of any kind exist there.
- Heaven is a place of love, light and positive energy and an oasis for the replenishment of the soul after it has returned home from its mission on Earth.
- Heaven is the soul's real home; a place of happiness, contentment, warmth and love. Earth life is a fleeting blip. When the soul returns home, it is as if it already knows this as its home and ultimate reality, but the soul forgets this on its return to Earthly life.
- Our true home is the spiritual world with God. We return there once we have fulfilled our earthly mission.
- Heaven is profound and expansive unconditional love, acceptance, joy, gratitude and understanding.
- Heaven is profound unconditional love, total acceptance and forgiveness.
- Heaven is unconditional love and acceptance, peace and happiness, and complete understanding.
- Heaven is knowledge, truth and love.
- Heaven is a spiritual place but also a state of mind; those who are able to experience Heaven on Earth are exceedingly blessed.

- Heaven is a place and a feeling of calm, profound peace, bliss, loving acceptance and being home.
- Heaven is ineffable. It is more of an emotion. It cannot be described in words adequately.
- Those in Heaven are neither aged nor frail nor disabled; they are perceived at their best moments. Those who died elderly appear younger; those who died as infants appear more mature.
- In Heaven, everything and everyone are singing praises to God. There is no time there. Everyone looks young and there are no sick people. Total peace and calm abide.
- Although our physical bodies may be aged and disease-ridden when we depart the earthly realm, our Heavenly soul-bodies appear younger and vibrant, happy and peaceful.
- Heaven has no Time as we know it on Earth.
- Heaven comprises radiant unearthly colors and buildings of luminescent glass crystal. They have apparent walls but their ceilings reach to eternity.
- Heavenly colors are alive, vibrant, glowing and pulsating.
- There is no sun in Heaven; only bright blue sky and intense light which is not harmful to the vision of the soul-body.
- Heavenly white light is alive, not hard on the eye, warm, welcoming and Home.
- I encountered the purest and whitest light I have ever seen. The bright light did not hurt my eyes and it was warm, bathing me in overpowering love and inner peace. It was absolutely wonderful.
- The brightness of the Heavenly light did not hurt the eyes or cause them to squint. The focus remained sharp, clear and precise. I saw many beautiful flowers of unearthly colors.
- The intensely clear and brilliant golden white light of Heaven is alive.

- The beautiful, living and uplifting Heavenly Light had its own identity.
- Heavenly light is filled with love and acceptance.
- Heavenly light is of ineffable brightness and nature; a light of Truth and Understanding.
- The Light is indescribably brilliant, radiant and beautiful. It does not impair the soul's vision. The love which emanates from the Light is indescribable, having no Earthly counterpart. The Light is perfect understanding and love.
- I found myself in a place of great magnificent "light." It was so beautiful and felt so wonderful. I felt so much love. It was indescribable. This pure love I have never experienced on this earth. It was different from the light on earth. I did not feel heat like the sun's rays nor did I have to shield my "eyes" from its intensity.
- The Light of Heaven is a calming, bright, unearthly, living, glowing and radiating essence.
- Heaven is bright and vibrant unearthly colors, and sweet, clear and fragrant air with a gentle warm breeze. There may be found singing birds, streams, trees, grass and flowers; there may be heard unearthly music more beautiful than any other. Each of these emanates its own sound and vibrations.
- Heaven is light, sound, joy, bliss and harmony. All around me were beings of consciousness, of pulsing, colored light and indescribable music and singing filled with joy and praise for God and All That Is. Heaven is our home.
- Nothing can compare on Earth with the Heavenly music I heard, comprising rich sounds blended perfectly together as one. Its mesmerizing beauty was experienced with the entire soul as wind or a sound-wave.
- Heaven consists of rolling fields of unearthly intense green, trees, birds, blue sky, gentle warm breezes, crystal

clear air and water, streams and soul-bodies in humanoid form.

- Heaven is vibrations and colors unseen on Earth.
- Heaven is not a gated community; it is open to all.
- Hell is the absence of God and the torment of the soul's own consequences. Hell is a place of fear and torment and absence of the presence of God.
- The three Beings of Light showed me Hell, but not the Hell that most people think. In fact, there is not a real Hell where bad people burn for eternity. Rather, Hell is a lack of God. The only Hell that we have to fear is a Hell of our own creation.
- Hell is being completely alone and without God.
- Hell is a state of being kept from the Light.
- Hell is your own conscience making you suffer for your misdeeds.
- I know now that "hell" is the fear that holds us. "HELL" is being stuck between the physical world and the next world. We need to have felt and understood the "love-of-being," that selfless, fear-less love at some point of our existence to pass that wall. That's the message of love, not the feeling most of us call love. There has to be nothing in it for us for our love to be pure (unconditional).
- I experienced my spirit leaving my body and being united with the "ultimate supreme spirit." I entered a place with a gathering of souls or spirits. I sensed great peace, tranquility and ecstasy – a rapture that was beyond a person's imagination. I felt as if I was a part of All, a part of God. I was mentally communicating and in sync with all, including not only some of my deceased acquaintances and relatives, but many of the Biblical prophets and great historical figures. I knew who everyone was. Every thought interacted with the whole community. I had no questions; it seemed as if everything was revealed and crystal clear.

- I was in a beautiful place. It was like a radiant, joyous landscape on a summer afternoon, but it was so much more – inexpressibly beautiful, serene and delightful with the most wonderful light pervading everything. Something like rolling hills with carpets of wildflowers. There were many beings there and they were blissfully happy. I was doing more than just seeing this; I was feeling it all with senses unimaginable. I knew these souls and they knew me. They radiated love and welcome. They were like family and we rejoiced in our reunion. It was rapturous. Although we didn't have physical bodies, we still "looked" the same, just more complete. Then a Being of pure light appeared – such an intense, beautiful white light, a thousand times brighter than the sun. I was drawn irresistibly towards it and was overwhelmed by the feeling of pure love and understanding which emanated from this wondrous entity. Nothing can describe it. This glorious entity recognized me, understood every minute aspect about me and poured love into me, which was real and immeasurable. I never wanted to leave this divine Presence but I was given to understand that I would have to return to my body.

- I was in the most beautiful place I have ever seen. I was near a beautiful blue lake that was as smooth as glass except for the two swans gliding through the water. At one end of the lake, a large willow tree leaned from the bank over the water. The grass was green and deep. The smell was that of a warm summer day, sweet and relaxing. Then I heard the music. It was music I have never heard before, beautiful and "angelic." I tried to distinguish the instruments, but I was unable to name them, and I realized the instruments did not have human names. Then the voices began, slowly at first, blending with the music until I could not distinguish the music from the voices. No voices spoke to me but my "soul" understood. The music and the voices were a lot like the wind in the trees, the kind of wind that soothes and caresses.

- I walked with a "friend" who was clad in a long white robe. He was beautiful. He had hair of gold and he shone of pureness, love, warmth and light. We walked together on green grass, alongside a pond as clear and blue as glass. In the pond were ducks and white geese swimming about without a care. The sky above was the softest, purest, warmest blue without a cloud in it. There were these amazing butterflies and birds flying about singing the most beautiful songs that I have ever heard. It was indeed Paradise.

- I found myself in the most beautiful place. There was a large tree shading the most incredibly green grass surrounded by flowers of every color, size and shape that ever existed. I heard a humming sound like a tone of some kind. I became aware of the individual sound each flower made. It was like each flower was very much alive and had its own personality by the tone that it made. All flowers together made a sound of perfection and harmony. I asked the Light in thought what was in the soil that would create such beautiful flowers. The Light answered, "Unconditional love." Every living thing, I was told, will find its own perfection with unconditional love.

Chapter 4

Interconnectedness/Oneness

On Earth we live in a dimension or realm of apparent separation and separateness. We perceive our world as full of separate physical objects and people. Our reality is one of dualism in which the observer is separate or removed from what is being observed. Each of us considers that we are separate from every other human being. We are separate from our pet animals. We are separate from the chair we sit on, the building we enter and the trees that surround us. But is that really so? Is that the true or the ultimate reality?

In Chapter 2, one of the recorded observations of a particular near-death experience stated that God is the energy of love that binds everything together and underpins all of the laws of physics. What could that possibly mean or entail? The notion that in the physical or material realm each of us is not really separate from each other or the chair we sit on or an adjacent tree seems at first blush quite incredulous and fanciful. But the concept of Universal non-dualism or oneness is beginning to emerge from recent research in the field of subatomic quantum mechanics/physics. The notion of separation and separateness is a complete illusion. According to particle theory, every object or thing is connected with every other object through energy and its vibrations. Each particle is connected to every other particle at the deepest foundational level of the Universe. And in the spiritual realm at least, the perceiver and the perceived cannot be separated, being indistinguishable.

It is interesting to note that this concept of interconnectedness/oneness has its religious counterpart in the Holy Scriptures of some religions like Judaism and Islam which emphasize that God/Allah is One. God is immanent in the sense of dwelling within each individual and connecting all that is. God is also omnipresent in the sense of being everywhere and in all things at the same time. And as numerous NDE descriptions documented in Chapter 2 observe, God is a universal energy permeating or running through all things and all of Creation.

From spiritual, religious and emerging scientific perspectives, each of us is intimately connected with everything in the Universe although we do not perceive, sense or appreciate this in the material/physical realm. As the following NDE observations suggest, that everything is connected to and part of everything else appears to be far more readily apparent in the higher spiritual realms.

- Everything is one. We are all connected.
- We are part of everything and everything is part of us.
- During my near-death experience, I was shown how we are all part of God and how God is a part of each one of us.
- Energy is life – it all comes from the same Source. We are all One, everything is One, past, present and future.
- Everything is connected although we cannot perceive it in our physical bodies. Everything in the universe is connected to everything else. We are Source energy; the essence of God.
- Energy is the single common component which connects everyone and everything.
- Seek first the Kingdom and Oneness of God. Separateness and duality are delusions of the Earthly realm.
- Experiencing the oneness of God is like awakening from an earthly dream of separation and dualism and feeling a sense of returning Home to the Ultimate Reality.
- Many souls and their experiences are one and one are many, both existing simultaneously in the same Time and Space.

- We are all connected to all life. We are at one with all living beings.
- I know now that we are all connected on this earth, in a way that perhaps we do not understand but we are.
- I can't explain what ALL ONE is but I know that we are all one.
- I returned from my near-death experience with the feeling that we are very much all connected and that the only thing that matters is LOVE.
- Although the soul is separate, it is one with the universes, galaxies, planets and life on Earth, and with all things seen and unseen. Like an intricate web, the soul is one with all consciousness and the Divine.
- Humans dwell in a world of separation and separateness but God is One in and with everything.
- While in the spirit realm, there was never a feeling of being isolated or alone. I experienced being at one with ALL – never separate.
- In the higher realms, we are not separate from the universal consciousness.
- I ceased to be separate and my consciousness became one with the Light.
- Outside my physical body, there was a profound realization of never being alone and always being in communion with other spiritual beings.
- Our souls are all one but retain their individual uniqueness.
- All souls are connected to the same Source, living different experiences.
- While outside my body, I experienced interconnectedness and oneness with everything in the universe.
- Outside of my body, I felt conscious but it wasn't part of my known Earthly reality. I felt such great peace. I had no sense of a body. It was just natural. It seemed like I was just floating around without any form in an expansive

reality where everything is all connected. I was just part of everything. I didn't really have a sense of "me." I was everything and everything was me. There was just "one."

- In the spiritual realm, all is interconnected.
- We are all one river.
- All things there (in Heaven) are in Oneness.
- To understand everything, the soul must merge with, become absorbed into, and become one with, the Light.
- In the higher realms, the "I" or ego does not exist. There is no separation or dualism.
- In the Light, dualism becomes oneness. We become Love itself and our Earthly identity dissipates.
- There is no "I." It is an illusion of the physical (earthly) realm.
- Relinquish your thoughts and ego and merge with the Light.
- We are all connected even though we erect barriers to separate, divide and protect us from our perceived and imagined fears and threats and to keep others from penetrating our lives. We are all linked to one another as children of God by our Creator. Therefore, we must care for and serve one another.
- We are one with everything; we are everything. We are love; everything is love. Everything is now.
- We are all one in the Universe. When we harm others, we harm our own soul.
- What is done to one is done to all. We are all one. Everything is one thing, made entirely of atoms. Humans, animals, the stars, things we can feel and touch are areas where the atoms are denser. It is not empty space between us but areas of less concentration of atoms. Therefore to hurt someone else is to hurt oneself.

- The smallest atom is the same as the entire universe. Everything is as small as the tiniest particle and as huge as the entire universe.
- All things are connected to each other and every part of the Universe is important in its own way.

Chapter 5

The Nature of the Soul-Consciousness

For thousands of years, philosophers, theologians and metaphysicists have pondered the question of what it means to be human and what we are comprised of. Are we more than our physical bodies? When our body dies, does our awareness end in an empty void of nothingness or does part of us continue in the form of what has been variously described as a soul, spirit, life-force or consciousness? And what is the relationship between such consciousness and the functioning human brain? Does consciousness depend exclusively thereon or is it transcendental in nature, existing outside of a functioning brain and indeed existing on a pre- and post-human experience basis?

Some of those who have undergone a near-death experience report some remarkable and definitive observations on these issues and questions. They observe consistently that our consciousness survives the death of our physical body and indeed does not depend upon a functioning human brain. Our consciousness survives the death of our body and brain. The brain merely serves as a conduit or filter respectively enabling and limiting access to universal knowledge, awareness and connection to the higher dimensions. As we shall see in Chapter 10 entitled "Our Earthly Life's Purpose and Meaning," this may be Divinely purposeful for enabling us to successfully complete our life's mission upon Earth. Consciousness is described as transcendental, limitless and eternal energy. Consciousness is our true essence, our mind, sense-perception, thoughts, feelings and emotions, and who and what we truly are at the deepest level of existence. It transcends all physical/material matter and is a foundational building-block of all that is and the Ultimate Reality. Outside of our physical body, our soul is a receptor to elevated awareness and expanded consciousness. Our physical bodies are mere temporary homes enabling us to pursue our Earthly mission.

What follows then are the most noteworthy written IANDS account observations that speak to these issues and offer revelations on the true nature of that aspect of the human being which I shall refer to as the soul-consciousness.

- The soul is conscious-energy.
- We are much more than flesh, bones and blood.
- You are more than your physical body; you are your spirit and this is the true reality.
- Our soul is energy, light, essence and consciousness. Our soul is infinite and eternal, transcending space and time.
- My near-death experience was a wonderful gift. I now know that consciousness exists beyond the physical body and that death is but a door we pass through.
- After my near-death experience, life is so much more precious to me. I believe that everything has spirit-consciousness.
- Our souls are light, frequency, vibrations and love.
- Pure consciousness is energy glowing with intelligence and love.
- Humans are an eternal soul in a physical body or shell experiencing life in a material realm known as Earth.
- Our consciousness is our soul which goes on forever and expands in the higher realms or dimensions. It is our eternal essence and is only housed temporarily in our bodies.
- The soul's temporary home is the physical body. The soul is the incorporeal and conscious aspect of human existence.
- The soul exists in a disembodied state in the higher realms.
- The soul-consciousness is more important than the physical body.

- As a result of my near-death experience, I no longer just believe but I know beyond doubt that we are so much more than our physical bodies. We are part of a larger body of consciousness. We can hardly even begin to comprehend and appreciate the beauty and complexity of our true nature as incredibly powerful spiritual beings.
- The events in our lives pass and are no more and will never happen again, but God and our souls are eternal.
- Outside of the body, consciousness and knowing awareness are vastly expanded.
- The soul's thoughts are crystal-clear in the higher realms.
- Although you can access consciousness with your brain, it exists outside the body. It is not contained in the brain. It is eternal and exists without a physical body.
- In truth, we never really sleep; only our bodies do. We are always aware and active on one level of consciousness or another. The fact that we dream while asleep is an indication of our consciousness always being active. Our bodies need to rest so that we can tap into and experience other aspects of our consciousness and being. The best way I can describe the transition from being "alive" on the physical Earthly plane and the passage to the Other Side is the passage from one room to another. You do not cease to be or lose consciousness; your consciousness simply shifts from one vantage point to another. Your outlook and feelings change. The feelings were profound and became that peace which surpasses all understanding.
- It is the essence, rather than the manifestation, of a person or thing which really matters and is the reality.
- Our thoughts are our essence.
- Our soul comprises the core essence within us that truly makes us who and what we are.
- Our consciousness is pure thought.
- Reconnect with the eternalness of your true inner nature.

- We are immortal because we have souls that never die.
- Our life does not begin and end on Earth.
- There is life after death, but this entails loss of your Earthly personal identity.
- The journey of our soul is an eternal learning and evolutionary process, interspersed between countless spiritual realms and physical incarnations.
- Remember who you truly are.
- The soul is a prisoner of the physical body and of the self. Relinquish your ego and enjoy expansive and liberated consciousness.
- Penetrate the depths of your consciousness to unlock the eternal Truths.
- Elevate your consciousness. Increase your vibratory rate.
- We simultaneously exist in more than one dimension of consciousness.
- Your soul is part of everything in existence all at the same time.
- In the spiritual realm, the essence of every consciousness is simultaneously experienced.
- You are simultaneously everything and nothing.
- The soul is male and female, it is love and joy.
- Every soul is special but no better or worse than others. The Light loves us all but we each have different paths.

Chapter 6

Liberation of the Soul-Consciousness

Albert Einstein once said that the true value of a human being is determined by the measure and the sense in which they have obtained liberation from the self. How may this be attained? Attachment is the greatest fabricator of illusions; ultimate reality can be attained only by someone who is detached (Simone Weil). We must therefore free ourselves as much as we can from the illusions and distractions of this Earthly plane.

How can we detach from this world? Spiritual and religious teachings and sages and seers have pondered this question for millennia. Detachment is separation from this world and all of its distractions and illusions. It is a letting go; an understanding of the relative unimportance and transient nature of personal power, fame and wealth. Detachment is a cessation of desire and craving, a suppression of one's covetous nature, ego and sensual appetites, and a loss of interest in worldly amusements, pleasures and self-preoccupation and self-identification. Detachment is a letting go of things which must be parted with in any event upon death. We enter this world with nothing and depart therefrom with nothing, apart from the treasures of, and love within, the heart and soul accumulated over a lifetime. In short, it is living a simple and uncomplicated life in the spirit rather than in the flesh. Liberation of the soul from these attachments produces peace, contentment and an elevation and expansion of consciousness or spiritual awakening.

Proceeding deeper within the higher spiritual realms entails a realignment of thought as to what really matters and what is real. It is like seeing for the first time; an opening of the mind to the limitless potential and possibilities that an abundant Universe has to offer us. Numerous accounts of those who have experienced a near-death experience point to various fallacious human constructs which have been deconstructed for them by their experiences in the higher realms. These include, among others, our human misunderstanding of the concept or notion of "death" associated with the demise of the physical body (to be discussed in more detail in Chapter 18), the limiting, restricting and constraining nature of social, cultural and belief systems on our ability to perceive eternal Truths and Universal Laws, and the irrelevance in the higher realms of our Earthly understanding of Time and its linear nature (to be discussed in more detail in Chapter 7). Fear is yet another illusion to be cast off. Some fear living while others fear dying. This fear may be so consuming that we fail to live our lives fully and authentically and remain oblivious to the purpose and meaning of life. And those who fear change in their lives should accept it as a natural effect and consequence of the workings of the Laws of the Universe. We must free ourselves from these illusions in order to recall the true nature of our soul-consciousness, what our purpose is on Earth and what our particular mission is in this lifetime. This is the path to self-realization and enlightenment.

Here are those comments and observations from NDE accounts which refer to the necessity to liberate and free the soul through detachment from the self and from fear.

- We are only as limited as we believe ourselves to be.
- We are much more than we ever believed ourselves to be.
- All of us have infinite potential; the Universe provides infinite possibilities for us. It is up to us to choose.
- There are no limitations; only limitless possibilities within you and surrounding you. Open yourself to the abundance of the Universe.
- Your mind is limitless. Do not be deluded by your finite physical body. We are unlimited spiritual beings.

- Humans have amazing potential and possibilities during their Earthly journey.
- The soul is subject to fewer limitations and restrictions than the physical body.
- Open your mind to the Universe and understanding will follow.
- The answers you seek are not to be found outside of you but all lie within you. Deconstruct all of the social and religious constructs you have accumulated during your lifetime and tune into the infinite and eternal Divine energy source within you.
- One's belief systems may be perceived in the spiritual realms to be severely limiting and constraining.
- Free yourself from the social and cultural codes and constructs you have accumulated.
- The concepts of right and wrong and good and bad are Earthly constructs and products of human perceptions. The concept of Hell is a human construct of Earthly control.
- There is nothing you can do wrong.
- "Dying" is a human-created Earth term or construct that means little in the spiritual realms.
- After my near-death experience, I have never been afraid of crossing over to the other side.
- I am not afraid of death now since I have seen a glimpse of the amazing realm that lies beyond.
- When you have gone beyond the veil and returned to your body, you will no longer fear death; in fact, you will long for it.
- Fear of death prevents many from living their life to the full and achieving their soul's mission.
- We are not alone. There is no reason to fear death.
- Accept your own mortality and embrace your eventual death. Release your fear of death and live a fuller life and feel more alive.

- Do not fear death and the unknown; upon re-birth in the spirit world, all-knowingness returns.
- Do not fear living or dying.
- There is nothing to fear. We are all Divine entities.
- Do not fear the unknown because your soul has always known that there is nothing which is unknowable.
- Everything in our life is fluid. Nothing remains the same. Every living thing grows and changes. Do not fear change. Let go of your security blanket as the Universe has more to offer than we could ever imagine. Accept change, let go and positive things will come your way.
- Time does not exist in the higher realms; everything happens at the same time. What we call the past and the future are mere human constructs.
- Time as we know it on Earth is just an illusion created by humanity; it simply does not exist. From the other side you can travel to any period of time.
- Infused all-knowingness imparted to the soul in the higher dimensions teaches the soul that there is no such thing as Time or Space.
- Unclutter your mind. Detach from the material world.
- Our souls cannot be truly liberated and enlightened and perceive the Universe wholly and accurately until they are liberated from the distractions and attachments of the world and all its illusions.
- Do not fill the empty void within you with the things of this world.
- The free (liberated) soul cares not for identity (ego) or wealth or fame. It does not carry the burden of worry or anxiety. It does not fear life on Earth or departure therefrom. This is what God calls us to become and why we are here on Earth.
- Extinguish your ego.
- Self-healing begins with our thoughts.

- Self-realization or enlightenment is the extinguishment of self and separation.
- Real beauty shines from deep within the soul. Unlike physical beauty which fades with time, real beauty comes from within and never fades. It is internal and eternal. Contentedness cannot be found without; it can only come from within our spiritual heart.
- A person's inner being is pre-speech and is more basic than emotions. It is your source of personal power and is your real self-identity. An adjustment to a person's inner being, however slight, can generate profound changes.
- Unlock the inner to rest and repose in eternity.

Chapter 7

Higher Spiritual Realms

The French philosopher Pierre Teilhard de Chardin once said that "We are not human beings having a spiritual experience. We are spiritual beings having a human experience." That we are much more than our physical bodies and that our core essence is spirit or soul-consciousness has been reiterated and corroborated by the many IANDS near-death experience accounts that were researched. On Earth we tend to preoccupy ourselves with physical and material self-gratification and seldom ponder the mysteries and grandeur and awesome nature of the unseen spiritual realms.

The world of spirit is beautiful beyond comprehension, and in their attempts to provide an accurate description thereof, the authors of the IANDS accounts have qualified these descriptions by using terms such as "ineffable" or "indescribable." There are countless universes, realms and dimensions, both seen and unseen, of vast complexity, some of which are intimately connected with the Earthly plane. The unseen spiritual realms of existence or being vastly outnumber the visible physical realms and exist alongside them.

Many of the following observations taken from the IANDS accounts are conceptually mind-boggling and virtually impossible to comprehend for those of us who have their feet planted firmly within this Earthly realm. It is not this author's remit to assess the correctness, truth or accuracy of these observations or concepts or to try to explain them. Rather, it is this author's task to accurately and fully report them as they were described in the reports and let the readers decide for themselves. All that is asked of the reader is to reflect thereon and maintain an open mind.

Those who have undergone an out-of-body experience comment on a number of themes and concepts concerning the higher spiritual dimensions which were revealed to them and which they experienced. A number state their firm and certain knowledge that reincarnation or transmigration of the human soul exists. That Beings of Light – guardian angels, spiritual guides and Ascended Masters – have accompanied and will accompany our souls throughout eternity. That outside of our body, we no longer experience pain and suffering but only peace and bliss. That negative energy such as hatred, anger, aggression, greed, fear, blame, judgment, pain, shame and suffering has no place in the higher realms including Heaven where only profound love, peace, understanding, forgiveness and acceptance may be encountered. That much of what we consider important in the Earthly realm is not considered as such within the higher realms. That our essence or soul is eternal and that our physical bodies are relatively insignificant and temporarily inhabited in order to pursue our Earthly mission or purpose and thereby evolve and prepare our soul for the higher realms.

In the higher realms, it is reported that communication is not verbal as we know it on Earth but rather like a form of telepathic communication in which thoughts, emotions, feelings and concepts are clearly, directly and instantaneously conveyed, transferred or shared between conscious beings. In the higher realms, there is no longer any sense of self or ego; our Earthly identities have been left behind and been replaced by vibrations and light by which we as souls and our evolutionary status are recognized.

Many experiencers are adamant that their experience in the spirit world was far more real than anything they have ever felt on Earth and are now dismissive of the Earthly notion that only that which is physical or material and visible to the eye is real. Some of the following observations remark that the soul is much less limited, restricted and fettered in the spiritual realm than it is in the physical realm. Its movement is freer in not being bound by temporal-spatial constraints. Sensory perception, particularly 360-degree panoramic vision facilitating vision in all directions, is richer and far more lucid. Once outside the body, the soul-consciousness is able to receive pure infused knowledge and understanding and to comprehend complex concepts much more quickly and deeply. And linear Time and Space as they are conceptually understood and experienced on Earth do not exist in the higher spiritual realms. One day is with the Lord as a thousand years, and a thousand years as one day (New Testament: 2 Peter 3:8 – King James Version).

What follows is an enumeration of the most impressive and insightful observations collated under various themes. The fact that different authors report remarkably similar observations should give us all pause to consider their plausibility.

On the Nature of the Spiritual Realms:

- The higher realms are ineffable in terms of human description.
- The spirit world is beautiful beyond comprehension.
- Love was everywhere. I was completely protected and safe. There was no question that everything would work out just as it should.
- In the higher realms, belief, faith and trust in God are superseded by a certainty of knowing, and awareness of, God.
- Everything takes on a different perspective in the higher realms.
- What we consider important in the earthly realm is insignificant and superficial (intranscendental) in the higher spiritual realms.
- The moments on Earth which seem so significant and profound pale in comparison with what we will experience beyond the veil.

- The cosmos is full of energy and vibrations and has countless realms, both seen and unseen.
- The soul-consciousness has a spiritual form contained in a small receptacle of transparent energy.
- The invisible spiritual world surrounds us, existing in dimensions of different vibrations and frequency rates. Our brains filter most of them out so we are unable to perceive them on Earth.
- There are an infinite number of realms of existence, part of the one Source, inhabited by beings beyond imagining.
- There are countless realms beyond realms, universes beyond universes, dimensions beyond dimensions: infinity.
- There are realms, dimensions and planes of existence, both seen and unseen, beyond the physical, material world.
- Spirit frequency vibrates at a higher level than the physical body.
- The physical world we experience is part of something vastly more complex.
- There is a very fine dividing line between the countless realms or vibrational planes of existence. Occasionally, the dividing line or veil is opened to allow interaction between them for a higher purpose.
- The unseen spiritual world exists adjacent to the physical, material world.
- We are spiritual beings having a human existence.
- Like human beings, spiritual beings also evolve. Although spirits may be at different levels of development, they remain on the same path to God.
- In order to spiritually evolve and graduate into the higher spiritual realms, we must learn to let go of our attachments to the current realm of existence we inhabit. These hold us back.

- In the spirit world, the soul-bodies of children who died continue to grow and evolve there.
- The physical body is the costume; the play is life on Earth. We are spirits using our body to learn and evolve.
- Empathy, understanding, forgiveness and acceptance allow the soul to progress to the higher realms.
- Your own spiritual evolution will automatically manifest to change your soul-bodily form.
- The tunnel leading to the Light is the soul's Heavenly umbilical cord.
- Physical death is the casting away of the body. You enjoy life in the earthly realm; super-life in the spiritual realms. A "cord" binds the body with the higher consciousness which is severed upon death.
- A life cord connects the physical body with immortal essence of consciousness which is severed upon physical death. It is shimmering, softly glowing, grey silk.
- From the perspective of the higher realms, our bodies are insignificant; their significance is only of the earthly realm.
- Earthbound spirits are those departed souls who refuse to enter the tunnel portal to follow the Light and so are trapped in the Earthly plane.
- The Beings of Light allowed me to see that when someone dies, they might be too attached to their Earthly existence to accept God's beauty, so they never go towards the Light. They get stuck "in-between," not accepting God and the Light.

On the Ultimate Reality:

- The spiritual realm is much more real than the physical realm, which is a transient illusion.
- My near-death experience was far more real than waking consciousness. This is so hard to explain. I was left with the conviction that a much greater reality exists for us beyond

this world. I had seen it, been in it. What had happened to me was real, I mean really real, as if normal life is just an illusion in which we are immersed for our time here. Our Earthly reality is a wondrous, awesome creation, and it has purpose, but a far greater reality exists.

- My near-death experience was similar to the feeling you have when you have been engrossed in a really good book for hours and then you put the book aside and notice the world around you. You had forgotten where you were and what time of day it was because the story held all your attention. You take a deep breath and notice the real world, even as you reflect on what you have been reading. Life is like the book, and having put it aside I could see and reflect on the whole story, gaining greater perspective on the ultimate reality.

- The ultimate reality lies beyond this life.

- Earthly life is our dream; spirit is our reality.

- When we dream at night, we do not consider it real but consider Earthly life to be our reality. But Earthly life is not real and is but a dream compared to the spiritual realms.

- What we dream at night is less real than our Earthly life which in turn is less real than the Ultimate Reality to be experienced in the Higher Realms.

- This side of the veil is like a movie and when the movie ends you leave the theatre and enter into the real world. When you die, you similarly leave the physical world and enter the real (spiritual) world.

- Strive more for the spiritual and less for the material and physical.

On Beings of Light:

- Our guardian angel has been with us from the dawn of time and will be with us for eternity.

- Every one of us has a guardian angel and spirit guide to assist our spiritual evolution throughout eternity.
- From the indescribable radiant light, a voice spoke to me. The voice was beautiful, calm, soft and loving.
- While out of my body, I heard a kind and gentle voice speak. Without my asking, the Voice in the Light answered all the big questions about life and my smallest concerns were addressed as if they were matters of great importance. The Voice had anticipated and joyfully fulfilled my needs and desires, with good humor, extreme love and enormous tenderness.
- Angels and spirit guides exist in the higher realms to watch over, protect and support us on our earthly journeys. We are able to connect with them with the proper intention and exercise of our Free Will.
- The more open we are to the possibility of help from the other side from our spirit guides, the more help we receive from them.
- I arrived in a very different place, in a very different state. There were others around me that I was aware of but I could not see them in the conventional sense. I had a sort of 360-degree awareness. There was another there with me, a guide, who was answering my questions. I knew that she was my guide on this side.
- We all have spiritual family whom our souls have always known but temporarily forgotten during our Earthly journeys. They are always watching over us and close to us and ready to assist us if that is what we wish.
- Loving and supportive spiritual beings are all around us even though we may not perceive them.
- In the spirit world, we are reunited with souls we have always known.
- In the spiritual realm, the soul is one with its surroundings and with every other being.

On Time and Space:

- The spiritual realm is nonlinear. There is no past, no future; only the present. Yet the present includes the future and the past. Everything that ever happened or is ever going to happen is actually happening at that very moment.
- There is no such thing as linear time on the Other Side. Everything is always experienced in the now, including past and future.
- Time and space do not exist in the higher realms which are folded and collapsed into oneness.
- The spiritual realm is timeless. Time does not exist as we experience it on Earth.
- Time does not behave in the spiritual realms as we are accustomed to on Earth. It is not really one thing following after another; rather, a moment can seem like an eternity and an eternity like a moment.
- In the higher realms, each moment is simultaneously a second and an eternity.
- Time has no meaning in Heaven.
- In the higher realms, Time does not constrain our soul.
- In the higher spiritual dimensions, Time and Space do not restrict the soul as they do in the Earthly realm.
- There is no such thing as Time. It becomes nonlinear in the spiritual world. It is only our human or earthly mind which makes Time linear. Your life – past, present and future – is happening simultaneously in the spiritual world.
- There is no past. There is no future. There is only now.
- There is no Time and Space. Everything simultaneously exists together in the higher realms.
- In the higher realms, the past, present and future (as we conceive them to be on Earth) are experienced simultaneously in a single moment.

- Every possible outcome for every possible situation is occurring at the same time, in the same instant.
- In the higher realms, you experience every possibility all at one instance.
- In the spiritual realm, the soul cannot sense Time. Time no longer limits or constrains.
- Higher realms are beyond the matrix of time and space.
- Time and space as we know these concepts on Earth do not apply in the higher dimensions.
- Time went on forever, but there was no time. Space went on forever, but there was no space. Time and space were one. Time and space did not exist.
- The concept of time is lost in the white light.
- I learned that time is meaningless in the higher realms.
- I was informed by my spirit guide that where I was, there were no time or space restrictions.
- Things are not as they seem in the higher realms. Time is not as it seems.
- Earthly time and space do not exist in the higher realms of spiritual existence.
- Time is only an illusion, made up to suit our Earthly experience.

On Negative Emotions and Feelings:

- Anger, greed and negative emotions do not exist in the higher realms.
- There is no fear, blame, judgment, pain or shame in the higher realms; only profound love, peace and unconditional acceptance.
- Struggles, challenges, worries and anxieties are part of the earthly realm; not of the higher realms.
- Out of your body, you feel no pain but only peace, contentment and serenity.

- Pain as we experience on Earth does not exist in the higher realms.
- No hatred, pain or suffering exists in the higher realms.

On Knowledge and Understanding:

- Pure and perfect understanding have they who experience the higher realms.
- For every question I asked of the Light, a complete answer was provided instantaneously. Perfect knowledge, understanding and awareness were imparted.
- In the higher spiritual dimensions, the soul receives instantaneous knowledge of how the physical and spiritual worlds operate and knowledge of everything there is to know about the universe.
- In the higher realms, there are no obstacles to awareness. Everything is instantly self-evident. If I turned my awareness to anything, it was self-evident to me with no delay.
- I experienced enormous clarity, understanding and knowingness in the higher realms.
- In the spirit world, understandings will come to you which you have always known but temporarily forgot while in the physical realm.
- Trust your intuition as that inexplicable knowing is based on knowledge derived in the spiritual realm.
- In the spiritual realm, knowledge and information are "downloaded" into your consciousness.
- A soul in the spiritual realm has full access to the universal data structure.
- In the higher spiritual realms, the soul reaches a higher level of consciousness and absorbs universal knowledge and insights through infusion, downloading or intuition.
- As the soul gains greater knowledge of the higher

dimensions, it can vibrate at a faster or higher level and can therefore access more and more information thereof.

On Expanded Sense-Perception, Vitality and Freedom of the Soul:

- In the higher dimensions, there is no pain and the soul is light and feels free of its captive body. Sensory perception is more in-depth and richer with a heightened sense of reality. Feelings and emotions are experienced more deeply.
- Thought and perception are clearer and more expansive while out-of-body.
- The senses of perception, particularly what we associate on Earth with seeing and hearing, are keener in the spiritual realms.
- In the higher realms, colors and sounds become more vivid.
- The soul-consciousness thinks and experiences more quickly and lucidly in the spirit world.
- The soul has 360-degree vision in the higher realms. I was able to see simultaneously in all directions.
- Out of my body I could see 360 degrees without turning my head.
- Upon death of the body, the soul-energy goes everywhere.
- The soul is less constrained and freer in the spiritual realm.
- Movement in the spiritual world is controlled by the soul's thoughts.
- To think of something in the higher realms is sufficient to move the soul-consciousness towards it.
- My new spiritual body was not subject to the law of gravity. If I wanted to go somewhere, I simply thought of where I wanted to go, and there I was.

- All I had to do was think of a location and I was immediately there.
- Wherever the soul wills to travel, it arrives virtually instantaneously.
- I was told that I could go anywhere at any time when I wanted by power of will. My spirit guide informed me that all I had to do was to think, to will a place and time and I would be transported there. I had all this power suddenly open to me in the higher dimensions.
- Movement of the soul-consciousness is not impeded by any limitations. Such movement is easy and instantaneous.
- Physical death liberates the soul into higher realms of consciousness where it can explore by thought and will.
- The soul can go anywhere in Time and Space because these concepts of the physical realm are not what they seem in the higher realms.
- The soul-consciousness can access any time or place on Earth from the higher spiritual realms.
- The spirit can simultaneously be at multiple places and times.
- As spirits we are unlimited, all-knowing and unfettered.
- In the spiritual dimensions, the soul's bodily form is restored and revitalized. For those who were vision- or hearing-impaired during their Earthly existence, their vision and hearing are restored.
- Soul-bodies look younger and healthier than when they departed the Earthly realm.
- Although the physical body may not have been at the time of death, the spiritual body is whole and vital. It appears younger although the physical body may have suffered the ravages of time on Earth. The spiritual body is not subject to aging by time as is the physical body on Earth.

On Communication:

- No words are spoken in the higher realms. All communication is telepathic. All questions are answered even before the thought question has been formulated.

On Identity:

- In the higher realms or dimensions, we have no Earthly name but are recognized by our vibration or light, our highest consciousness.
- In the spiritual realms, there is no sense of time or self.
- Earthly matters we associate with our self or ego dissipate and are meaningless in the higher realms.
- While we are known in the Earthly plane by our birth name, we have a different name in the spiritual realm.

On Reincarnation:

- Outside of my body, I learned that reincarnation of the soul is a universal law.
- We have many past lives. Only the body dies; the spirit/ soul was made for an eternity. We have all passed through many lives. Our soul-energy cannot be destroyed.
- My out-of-body experience imparted to me that I have lived on Earth many times before.
- I was shown in great detail the choice of reincarnation.
- My belief in reincarnation and karma has been strengthened by my out-of-body experience. I now have certain knowledge and proof thereof.
- Death of the physical body is a prelude to the soul-consciousness undergoing a life-review to reflect on

what it learned from that lifetime to prepare for its next incarnation.

- The quality of person that you are in this life directly affects your quality of life in the next phase of your evolutionary journey.
- We keep coming back until we have learned all of the lessons and get it right.
- Souls are reincarnated and can be either sex in previous lifetimes.
- As a result of my near-death experience, I now believe in reincarnation.
- After every life we live we become stronger and truer, tempered by our experiences until such time as we may complete our journey and we are truly born.

Chapter 8

Universal Metaphysical Knowledge and Understanding

How impossible it is for humanity to understand, beyond the most basic and rudimentary level, the spiritual realms, as humanity has been given only a little knowledge thereof by the Creator (Qur'an 17:85). That this is so may well be related to a higher purpose, to enable each of us to successfully achieve our Earthly purpose or mission and to thereby evolve into the higher spiritual realms (to be discussed in greater detail in Chapter 10). While human knowledge and understanding of the seen material physical realm we call Earth have been accumulating for millennia, we are only on the threshold of a greater and more profound understanding of the unseen spiritual realms and dimensions. We are squarely located within the realm of metaphysics – study and research into that which cannot be learned, at least at this point in history, through objective study of material reality; a postulated reality outside of human sense perception. But this may well be changing with recent advances in quantum mechanics physics and medical and scientific research into the near-death experience phenomenon.

Divine/Source/Universal understanding is not the same as human understanding. A prodigious gulf separates them; only the former can enlighten or awaken or remind the soul. Understanding is perceiving the way things actually are as opposed to the way we perceive them to be; observing each phenomenon in its true nature as it actually is, rather than through the prism of material illusion, the attachment of labels or names, or through the cultural-religious filter of one's lifelong accumulated individual preconceptions and conditioning.

Many of those who have undergone an NDE report that once outside the body, they receive instantaneous knowledge and awareness. They use various terms to describe what happens to them in this regard, including "osmosis," "downloading," "infusion," "plugging in" or "wired in." They become aware of how the physical and spiritual worlds operate and interact with each other and gain an instantaneous understanding of conceptually difficult, complex and challenging matters that would take much longer on Earth to absorb and comprehend. Some report that the received knowledge is that which has always been known by the soul-consciousness but temporarily forgotten during its Earthly incarnation. A certain level of knowingness or omniscience is attained whereby certainty and proof henceforward replace trust and faith. I no longer believe because I now know (referring, for example, to the existence of God/the Source, Heaven, Beings of Light, the purpose of our life on Earth and reincarnation). They also receive God's assurances that we are never alone and that each of us is loved and held precious beyond human comprehension by Our Creator.

The Buddha once said that in order to fully understand, we have to become one with what we want to understand. And those who seek God understand all things (Proverbs 28:5). Here then is what those who have undergone an NDE have to say about universal knowledge, awareness and understanding.

- Humanity is only just beginning to understand Creation.
- Towards the Universe have a childlike wonder and curiosity and a desire to learn and understand its mysteries.
- Hunger and thirst for knowledge, particularly of the spiritual.
- Hoping for something or having faith in something is not as reassuring as knowing it, as when you return from beyond the veil.

- The knowingness I received from the infused universal knowledge while outside my body is higher than hope and faith.
- As a result of my near-death experience, belief/faith was superseded by knowingness and certainty.
- There are some things we as humans do not and cannot understand for a higher purpose. We cannot and do not understand everything in the earthly realm because we are not supposed to.
- The Universe will guide you and give you understanding, but the soul must remain alert, open and receptive.
- Outside of your physical body, the soul has an instant connection with Divine knowledge and all of its questions will receive instantaneous answers.
- Knowledge of anything I wanted to know was instantly transferred without language.
- I was completely in awe of the beauty of the pure love I was being surrounded by. One of my greatest memories is that of all knowledge being available. If I had a question in my thought, I immediately had the answer.
- In the higher realms, there is no such thing as a question without an accompanying answer. All answers are provided instantaneously, clearly and completely.
- During my experience, I was downloaded with information about every question I had ever had. I received instantaneous knowledge of everything there is to know.
- In the spirit world, we receive infused knowledge and understanding.
- I knew and understood how everything worked, the laws, if you will, of that higher dimension.
- I automatically knew things and accepted them without fear or hesitation. It was normal for this new dimension I was now in.

- My soul was plugged into expanded knowledge and awareness, making sense of all of the mysteries of the Universe.
- I emerged from my near-death experience with a total understanding of the machinations of the universe and the phrase "Love is the answer; communication is the key."
- I was given knowledge of many things on different levels, appearing instantaneously in my mind. It's as if the knowledge of the ages all appeared in my mind at once.
- My spirit observed the entire history and evolution of the Universe as if in a fast-forward film.
- I became acutely aware of the immeasurable vastness of the Universe and I knew what Eternity was.
- Knowledge is imbued into the soul in the higher realms.
- Infused knowledge from the higher realms is simple and logical; it is humans which are prone to over-complication.
- Divine knowledge and eternal Truths are simple to understand; the complexity and difficulty are in the living of them during our earthly existence.
- The knowledge of the Universe is deceptively simple and apparent and yet in the earthly realm we have difficulty remembering it or perceiving it. This knowledge is filtered out before we are born to enable us to learn and grow from our earthly experiences.
- The white energy of God creates within our soul a knowledge which makes all things clear.
- The Light of God infuses the soul with the depth and breadth of eternal knowledge and the wisdom of the ages.
- You will eventually understand everything and all Truth.
- Death of our body is the extinguishment of our earthly identity and ego, replaced by omniscience and total understanding.
- The soul understands everything in the higher realms.

- Upon leaving the body, the soul acquires knowledge of everything. A question is instantaneously answered. You become part of the infinite pure white light.
- In the spiritual realm, the soul is one with its surroundings and with every other being, sharing all the information and knowledge there is to know.
- The collective consciousness comprises the experiences of all who ever lived, the collective knowledge of all. These collective experiences are omniscient knowledge. Everything that has been thought, spoken and done has been recorded. (Author's Note: This would possibly be akin to the so-called Akashic Records.)
- All religions have been created by Humanity to try to understand what truly cannot be fully understood during this earthly existence.
- I was given knowledge that the Universe is unfolding as it should.
- Upon reaching the opening at the end of the dark tunnel, I experienced the Light, a huge white glow which was massive in size. It was pure, non-judgmental, loving and accepting. Tremendous knowledge was given to me, yet it was not the sort of knowledge you acquire from reading books. It was more like Enlightenment or a meeting with God.

Chapter 9

Communication in the Spiritual Realms

Some of the IANDS written accounts mention the nature of communication within the spiritual realms. Most authors agree in consistently describing such communication as basically telepathic in nature but that it is more than that. That although telepathic communication is the best way to describe or explain it in terms of human or earthly language, it goes beyond that.

It is essentially instantaneous and direct nonverbal or wordless communication or sharing of knowledge; an unspoken dialogue between soul-consciousnesses. The communication is much quicker and more lucid than upon Earth and, unlike the earthly plane, there is no possibility of any misunderstanding or misinterpretation. Nothing is lost in translation. It is much more than instantaneous thought transfer, however. It also includes the relaying or transfer of concepts, ideas, knowledge, events and images, accompanied by associated feelings and emotions. The communication is said to be to the deepest core of our consciousness or being. The accounts observe that it is nothing like anything they have experienced upon Earth. Concepts, ideas and universal laws which are difficult to comprehend upon Earth are understood instantly and with ease in the higher spiritual realms.

Here is what those who have undergone a near-death experience have described in relation to the nature of consciousness-to-consciousness communication within the spirit world.

- Everything is communicated by thought. Questions are answered even before the thought is completed.
- I was communicating with the Light telepathically. There wasn't really a dialogue. The thought just formed in my

mind. But I knew the instant the thought formed that the Light was able to know and understand.

- Spiritual communication is nonverbal and instantaneous. It involves relaying entire concepts and events with associated feelings and emotions.
- I communicated with the Being of Light through mental telepathy, which is faster and more efficient than mere words.
- Communication was really different, as I didn't speak. I felt thoughts welling up inside of me and my questions were answered immediately. There were no words, it seemed that it was all feeling, all intuitive.
- Communication occurred through instantaneous osmosis, rather than by human verbalization.
- I had much conversation with the Light without any words being spoken.
- I became aware of a Buddha-like entity who communicated to me by thought.
- In the Light, I walked/floated and talked with two spiritual beings. Our talking was done by thinking, not by our mouths.
- Thoughts are communicated telepathically through our spirit/soul and are felt emotionally and spiritually. It is communication from consciousness to consciousness.
- In the spiritual realms, thoughts are registered in the mind without words being spoken. Images and feelings are directly communicated.
- No physical words or sounds were exchanged; only a direct and lucid transfer of thoughts, ideas and concepts from consciousness to consciousness.
- I could not "speak" or "hear" like the physical body on Earth but I could "speak" and "hear" in a spiritual sense just the same. It was like telepathy.
- Spiritual communication is consciousness-to-consciousness unspoken dialogue or mental

communication. It is an instantaneous thought process which does not rely on hearing or voice. It is associated with feelings of peace, understanding and acceptance.

- While out of my body, everything communicated was telepathic like energy thoughts being exchanged. The communication was fast.
- You think the thoughts and they are automatically communicated. Unlike Earth, there is no misunderstanding or misinterpretation of what you are trying to say. Spirit-to-spirit communication is akin to soul mates or identical twins. Spiritual communication is a profound experience.
- Each time I thought of a question, the answer was returned instantly and profoundly.
- Thoughts, feelings and concepts are conveyed to the deepest core of our consciousness.
- Telepathic communication may not be the best description of spiritual communication but it is essentially the instantaneous direct exchange of knowledge and thoughts.
- In the spirit world we communicate through our hearts and feelings so that there could never be any misunderstanding.
- In the spiritual realms, the mind of the soul-consciousness knows exactly what other spiritual beings are thinking. Physical voices and sounds are not heard. Spiritual communication involves a direct transfer of thoughts in such a clear manner that there is no possibility of misunderstanding.
- Communication in the world of spirit is like a direct transfer of thoughts with no possibility of misunderstanding.
- It was disclosed to me that in humanity's future, written and spoken words will no longer be necessary.

Chapter 10

Our Earthly Life's Purpose and Meaning

What is the meaning of life? What is the purpose of our life on Earth?

Many of us never really consider these questions, at least not beyond a superficial level. We may not have any interest in them or we may not have the time required to properly consider them. There are many distractions and amusements in life that take us away from these important questions. We may have financial pressures concerning payment of our mortgage and bills, workplace stresses, family responsibilities as well as time constraints. We may be looking to sculpt the perfect body and to pursue other self-adornments. We may be news junkies or addicted to social media or otherwise spend an inordinate amount of time being lost in cyberspace. And yet this is very much a part of our contemporary life and who we are.

And when we do find time and space to ponder these fundamental questions, we may tend to look too deeply at them, dissect them too finely and perhaps over-think or over-complicate them. But the answers to these questions, gleaned from beyond the veil by those who have undergone a near-death experience, are strikingly and disarmingly simple, although the living out of them in this Earthly realm within the context of our everyday interactions may be more difficult and challenging.

What, then, are the answers to these questions sourced from beyond the veil? The IANDS accounts deliver a uniform message in this respect. Essentially, we are here to learn and to love and be loved; to develop loving and caring relationships. We are here to expand within ourselves our capacity for unconditional love – a love that neither demands nor expects anything in return – and to manifest it towards other beings. All of us will eventually be asked how loving, caring and kind were our thoughts, words and actions during our time on Earth (see Chapter 19 on our Life-Review).

Many interesting insights concerning these questions are offered up in the various IANDS accounts surveyed. Life is a precious gift and all of us have a reason for being here. We each have an individual and tailored mission which may seem relatively modest by the standards of the contemporary world but for each soul it is very significant. We are to live life to the full and to derive joy from our experiences and relationships on Earth. We are here to explore and to learn; life is our teacher and our individual experiences are our classroom. It is natural and inevitable for us to make mistakes for such is the human condition. But we are expected to learn from our mistakes and thereby to develop strength and beauty of character and spirit. Although we may not realize it at the time, things and events happen in our life for a reason. There is meaning and a higher purpose in everything. There are no coincidences in life; everything happens according to a Divine plan which you have been co-opted into creating for the spiritual development of your soul prior to your birth in the Earthly plane (for more detail, see Chapter 11 on "Soul Agreements"). Challenges, struggles, trials and tribulations are a necessary part of our soul's learning experience on Earth to enable us to develop patience and perseverance and to rise above our suffering. We are to trust our intuition and inner awareness and follow the dictates of our conscience and spiritual heart. But above all, we are to serve God by loving and assisting others, both materially and spiritually. We are to become selfless rather than selfish and to carry within our hearts the Divine virtues of gratitude and forgiveness. We are to search within ourselves for who we truly are and to realize our considerable potential concerning what we can become.

Here is what has been brought back from beyond the veil by the authors in their own words in relation to why we are here.

- During our Earthly lifetime, our mission is to make a difference.
- How we live our life is what matters.
- Make sure you give more than you take.
- Everything that life brings is beautiful and for a higher purpose, although we may not consider it so at the time.
- Life is beautiful but we too seldom notice.
- Life in the earthly realm is a soul journey and venturing forth to learn; physical death is a returning home for the soul's rest and debriefing before its next incarnation.
- Life is a journey or adventure for our soul. Through the exercise of our gift of Free Will, we can make of it whatever we will.
- I understood that I was here (on Earth) to learn and to grow (should that be what I chose to take from my earthly experiences).
- The experience we call life is only transitory. It is a place of preparation, of choices, of opportunities to grow.
- Learning continues throughout eternity. The soul's destiny is to seek to acquire universal knowledge both in its Earthly incarnations and in the afterlife.
- Each Earthly lifetime is a chapter in a book detailing our soul's evolutionary journey. During the living of each lifetime, we sometimes forget who we truly are but the recollection returns when we depart our physical body and return Home to Heaven.
- Physical death is a reunion with all that our soul loves, a going home. It is something to look forward to after a lifetime of learning, being positive and loving towards others and taking joy from our life.
- Our purpose here is to discover unconditional love within ourselves and then offer it to others. We are all on the same path but choose different life experiences. No one path is more important than another. It is all a

matter of what resonates with your heart. We are here to explore, experience and find joy in our earthly existence. Our ascension as a spirit happens at a time we are ready to receive it. We are all constantly evolving. We are all spiritual beings having varied human experiences.

- Our Earthly experiences are training for the highest levels of Heaven.
- The world we live in is our school.
- I understood from the Light that Earth is a school and when we are finished we take a final exam (the life-review) and then we get to graduate and go back home (to Heaven).
- The lesson is so simple. It's all about love. Understanding how much God loves us and how well we love ourselves and others.
- Consider every obstacle in your life as a challenge and an opportunity to discern the particular lessons you were sent to Earth to learn.
- Some of us are here to teach, some to learn and some to do both.
- The only thing that matters in your life is how loving your thoughts and actions are.
- It is the selfless things we do for others out of unconditional love that really matter.
- Live for God and for others.
- Live Heaven on Earth.
- Perceive God in others and reflect that love back to them.
- Perceive everyone and everything in a new spiritual light.
- The most important thing in life is love.
- Cultivate a profound and boundless love and acceptance for others and all beings.
- Life on Earth is about loving relationships. All you can carry with you upon your physical death is the love you have given others.

- The energy of love is the essence of life.
- All we need and can give in this earthly life is love.
- You are on Earth for only one reason: to love and help each other.
- Love one another and be kind to each other.
- Arguing and fighting are not what God intends for us. We are meant to try to be a good person and love and help each other.
- We all have a purpose, to help others and not to judge them.
- Find peace and satisfaction through helping others.
- The more we help others, the better will be our soul journey.
- Love all and forgive. This is the essence of our earthly life and learning.
- We are here to love and be loved. Savor and learn from your life experiences.
- We are here to love each other and learn.
- Trust your instincts, follow your heart and soul, listen to your inner true self, live your life in alignment with your life's purpose and share your light and love.
- Our Earthly life is not meaningless although we may experience difficulty in perceiving its meaning.
- There are no coincidences; everything happens for a reason.
- There is meaning in everything.
- Every trivial event has actual meaning and everything happens for a reason.
- There are meaning and purpose in everything.
- There is a reason for and behind everything.
- All things happen for a reason; nothing is random in the Universe.
- Each life experience has a higher purpose and helps us to achieve our life's mission.

- We come to Earth to learn.
- Life is short so enjoy it.
- Life is a precious gift from God. All of us have a reason for being here.
- Our time on Earth should be treasured and respected.
- Earth is temporary. Love is the message of our earthly life.
- Derive joy from your earthly life. Do not be concerned over what others may think of you.
- We exist on this earthly plane to struggle, to learn, to live our life authentically to the full, to spiritually evolve, to serve God, to assist other souls in their spiritual evolution and to add something of value to the world.
- One needs to ponder what things are preventing us from living our earthly life to the fullest. We need to change ourselves accordingly.
- Live your life to the full and your life's mission will be fulfilled.
- Life is meant to be lived in abundance.
- We are here to learn, make mistakes and to grow, to serve humanity, to be less self-centered and to do acts of kindness ungrudgingly and not expecting anything in return.
- It is not about what you materially possess, but what you have given to others.
- Hold the light and energy of God and share it with others.
- We are here to learn and teach and help one another. We continuously and eventually evolve into the companions we were created to be for God.
- Our Earthly purpose is to learn and teach unconditional love, compassion and forgiveness.
- We reconnect with who we truly are and where our souls have come from through manifesting love and compassion towards others.

- Help others to heal their wounded spirit.
- My near-death experience taught me that my purpose is simply to heal myself and to help heal other people and restore their natural state. We as humans are so out of balance and we need to restore that balance to achieve our full potential.
- Evolve your spirit while in your transient and mortal body.
- Earth is a restricted, limited and difficult plane of existence.
- The meaning of life is to struggle and through that struggle to learn. Life is the teacher; our classroom is our experiences.
- Life is replete with struggles and challenges, but that is the way it is supposed to be; to enable us to learn and persevere.
- This life is a series of lessons and challenges to strengthen our spirits and expand our capacity for unconditional love.
- Trials, tribulations and struggles are essential for our soul's development and evolution.
- Regardless of the struggles and challenges we face in life, they are temporary and fleeting but necessary for the evolution of our soul-consciousness.
- Emotions, worries and challenges are part of our earthly journey.
- Struggle and pain are not to be feared; rather, they are opportunities for the soul to learn, grow and evolve.
- Suffering allows us to overcome and grow.
- Through pain and suffering come greatness and nobility.
- The lot of humans is to experience the full range of emotions so that we may feel our earthly journey and better learn and grow from it.
- Persevere until the end.

- Your purpose is what you say it is. Your mission is what you set for yourself. Your life is what you create for yourself and no one will stand in judgment but you.
- Do not be overconfident in planning your life journey. Humans may propose but God disposes. There are no coincidences. Everything happens according to a Divine plan which you have been co-opted into creating prior to your birth.
- Each one of us comes to Earth for a purpose.
- We each come here with a mission but most of us forget or ignore what that mission is. Our mission may be relatively modest by the standards of the world but for each soul it is most significant.
- The experience of this earthly life is but a dream, a life plan or programming that we all undergo so that we may learn what we need to know and evolve into the essence of what we truly are.
- We are here on Earth by choice to fulfil our soul's life purpose. We are unique and precious to God. We are only expected to love, and be of service to, others, through exercise of Free Will.
- Remain alert to people who come within your life path; Divine messages may be conveyed to you in different and unexpected ways.
- Do not fret over petty things.
- One day it will dawn upon you that all of your life's experiences have brought you to where you are now.
- What we truly long and search for on Earth cannot be found in this plane; but only in the higher realms with God.
- Victory or defeat, worldly success or otherwise, it is all the same; for when we transition beyond the earthly realm, the only thing that really matters is how we treated and related to others.

Chapter 11

Soul Agreements

As we learned in the previous chapter, each of us has a role to play in the Divine plan and each of us comes to Earth for a reason. Prior to birth in the Earthly realm, the soul voluntarily chooses its Earthly incarnation and accepts certain tasks or mission to be completed during its lifetime in order to serve God and to elevate or evolve the soul-consciousness. In consultation with Beings of Light, including angels and spirit guides, the soul chooses the family and parents it will be born into, the location and circumstances of birth, the length of the Earthly life, and the life lessons to be learned during the lifetime in order to maximize the chances of successfully completing the tasks and mission. This agreement of life plan then permits the soul to experience life in whatever form it has chosen and there is virtually little or no opportunity for the plan to be changed, at least unilaterally by the soul.

Upon birth on Earth, the soul leaves behind a state of all-awareness or omniscience, and forgets much of the Universal Knowledge it absorbed in the higher realms as well as who and what the soul truly is. The soul also forgets its previous incarnations and the tasks or mission for this lifetime which it had previously chosen in consultation with the Beings of Light. As life on Earth continues and worldly distractions and concerns increase, the soul is unable to realign itself with these important matters unless and until it raises its awareness or consciousness of Universal Knowledge and Divine Virtues, thereby realigning itself with its true self or essence and its sacred mission. Once this is achieved, completion of the tasks and purpose or mission is facilitated to a much greater degree. These are the rules and how life on Earth is meant to operate.

Some of these observations are borne out by the teachings of the ancient Greek philosopher Plato. According to him, the soul enters the body at birth from a higher realm of existence. At birth, the soul leaves a state of all-awareness behind for a less aware or conscious earthly state and forgets many of the eternal truths and universal knowledge which are imbued into the soul in the higher realms. Death of the physical body (or spiritual re-birth) is a remembering of, or reawakening to, all or most of what the soul had forgotten or had erased before its birth into the Earthly plane.

It is interesting to note that from an Eastern philosophical or metaphysical perspective, *The Tibetan Book of the Dead* offers a counterpart or analogy to what has just been described. In the so-called "Bardo of Becoming" just prior to physical birth in the Earthly realm, we are allowed to choose the continent of our birth. And in the "Bardo Prayer which Protects from Fear," a supplication is made that when we see our future parents in union, we are allowed to see the peaceful buddhas with power to choose our birthplace for the good of others.

The following observations are taken from those NDE accounts which referred explicitly or implicitly to the concept of the soul agreement.

- We are all loved and from the same Source, experiencing life in whatever form we chose before birth.
- Before we are born into the physical/material realm, our soul chooses the family into which we are born, the parents who will raise us, the lessons we are to learn during our lifetime, and when we shall exit our earthly existence and graduate from the earthly University of Life. We make those choices in a predetermined way to maximize our learning opportunities.

- During my life-review, I was shown why I had the parents I had. I had asked for them before birth so that I could learn what I needed to learn on Earth.
- Prior to our physical birth, the soul voluntarily accepts certain tasks or mission to serve the Love and Light that is God to be performed during one's earthly lifetime.
- The communication with the Light concerned my prenatal chosen human life's work.
- We are here on Earth by choice to fulfil our soul's life purpose.
- Your (life's) mission is what you set for yourself.
- We choose our Earthly life and our parents before we are born. We each have a role to play which is essential for our development and evolution. Struggles are essential for that to happen.
- While out of my body, I was told that my life would only last for the time that was planned by destiny. Almost nothing of what was planned could be changed.
- While outside my body, I remembered the time prior to my birth. I was in a huge dimly lit room. A voice called out to me and I went towards it. The voice came from a radiant Light. The voice communicated to me that it was my turn to go down and give humanity a message from God that He is alive and well. The next thing I knew I was being born.

Chapter 12

The Gift of Free Will

Free Will is a precious gift or privilege which is bestowed upon each of us by God/The Source. We have the freedom or autonomy to make decisions for ourselves which affect us in our daily living, ranging from personal health and well-being issues to our jobs, careers, relationships with others and what we believe. As such, Free Will plays a most significant part in our lives and how we live. As we observed in Chapter 11, although the overarching aspects of our Earthly lifetime are already determined through the soul agreement (such as when, where and to whom we are born, our date of death and our life tasks and mission), our particular life experiences are chosen by us. As some of those who have undergone a near-death experience observe, God honors and respects all of the choices and decisions we make for ourselves but we remain responsible for them at the soul level (which we shall later discuss in Chapter 19 entitled "Our Spiritual Re-Birth and Life-Review").

Why are we each granted Free Will? Perhaps we can borrow from a domestic or family analogy. As loving and caring parents who want the best for their children, we allow them increasing autonomy and independence to make their own decisions as they mature and their decision-making capacity evolves. However, we know as parents that they will sometimes make mistakes (as we all do), but we hope and indeed expect that they will acknowledge, accept responsibility for, and learn from their mistakes and thereby grow and mature into responsible adults. Similarly, God allows us to find our way or to blunder through life by letting us make our own choices when we reach the proverbial fork in the road. The choices we make either help us to achieve our soul's mission in life or take us further away from it. Sometimes we must fall and pick ourselves up again for our souls to learn and grow. And sometimes sadly, we do not learn and develop total amnesia concerning why we are here and what we are supposed to do. But making mistakes and suffering the consequences therefrom help us to learn and evolve and align with our Earthly mission.

God does not want to force us to love Him or to force us to strive after Divine virtue or righteousness. Of course, He wants that to be so but to force us to do so would not be genuine, authentic, honest or pure. God wants us to be spontaneous and genuine rather than grudging. He loves us so dearly that He allows us to make a choice between growing towards Him or falling away from Him. Free Will can, of course, be exercised for positive or negative purposes or, to put it into the language of the Abrahamic religions and Eastern metaphysical philosophy respectively, good and evil or wise/enlightened/awakened and ignorant. Negative energy, evil and ignorance do not exist in the higher realms but are necessary in the Earthly realm to enable our souls to make important Free Will choices. Our cumulative life choices will either facilitate a growth and evolution of our soul-consciousness towards God or a falling away from the Light and consequent misalignment with our Earthly mission.

Free Will is vital to pursuing and succeeding in our Earthly life's mission and in facilitating our ascendance into the higher spiritual realms. Our purpose here on Earth is to grow towards the Divine but we can just as easily fall away depending on how wisely or ignorantly we have exercised our gift of Free Will. For those who actively pursue and live by the positive energy of the Universe, there is great reward; for those who choose to pursue negative energy, there is forgiveness and an opportunity for redemption (see Chapter 17 for a discussion of, and observations on, positive and negative energy). The exercise of our gift of Free Will in such a manner as to resist negative energy and utilize positive energy in the living of our life facilitates an elevation and expansion of our soul-consciousness.

Many of us perceive ourselves to be "victims" of life and what it throws at us, and this term seems to be gaining increasing currency in contemporary dialogue. Admittedly there are many things and circumstances in our life which lie largely beyond our control. But as a number of those authors who have recorded their near-death experience attest to, all too often we are also victims of the way in which we have exercised our Free Will through unwise or ignorant decision-making which has drawn too much on negative rather than positive energy.

Here then are some of the observations and insights made on Free Will by the authors of those IANDS written accounts studied.

- God is unconditional love and gives us the gift of free will to make our own choices.
- Free will to create our own earthly reality is the greatest gift we are given.
- We are given opportunities in life and we have free will to make choices.
- Each of us has the power to change our course through free will.
- Although our Earthly life is predetermined on one level, its course may be changed by the exercise of Free Will.
- We determine our own path by exercising our free will and making decisions when arriving at forks in our personal path.
- Everything you have done and all you have been through were to prepare you for the juncture in your life right now. We are free to choose from among many forks in our path. But with such freedom comes responsibility, so choose wisely.

- You are the author of your own destiny. No one else can write your story.
- We are the creators of our own universe.
- Life is not a series of coincidences but of choices made, the consequences which we remain responsible for at the soul level.
- God honors all choices we make pursuant to our free will. He will not veto our choices but we remain accountable to our Higher Selves for those choices.
- Each soul has the free will to choose its own destiny, to choose between positive and negative energies, but the universal laws are such that the soul has to face the effects of what it chooses.
- One of the greatest gifts given to humans is free will.
- The gift of free will or choice is a great gift, but decisions should be made from our soul heart to secure the greatest good overall.
- Human free will is that part of our soul that is able to render positive service to the Universe if it so chooses. That free will can also be exercised for negative purposes.
- Our experiences are what we choose through exercising our free will.
- It is our privilege to be granted Free Will. We decide and make choices. So how then can we feel that we are a victim?
- Do you consider yourself a victim? Aren't we all? Focus rather on what you want going forward and your past will fall away. You are the designer and author of your destiny.

Chapter 13

Loving Yourself

We must love ourselves not in a narcissistic sense but in a compassionate sense.

We can be prevented from living our life to the full, experiencing spontaneous joy and succeeding in carrying out our life's mission if we are constantly judging ourselves and being self-critical; believing that we are unworthy and insignificant in the vast scheme of things and feeling guilty over what we have done or not done. If you despise or disrespect yourself or otherwise suffer from a lack of self-esteem, it will be difficult for you to see the good and God in others.

As rain falls equally on the just and unjust, do not burden your heart with judgments but rain your kindness equally on all (Buddhist teaching). And this includes being kind and gentle to yourself. Beyond a wholesome discipline, be gentle with yourself (*Desiderata* verse 15). Although we should strive to maintain a healthy self-discipline, we must also not be too hard on ourselves. We should therefore not judge ourselves too harshly, which many are prone to do. As a child of God, each of our souls is unique and deeply loved and cherished in Heaven; therefore accept your imperfect self for who and what you are, all the while striving to become the best possible version of your Higher Self.

Imperfection affects us all but God loves and accepts us perfectly. Here is what the authors of the NDE accounts have had to say on the importance of each of us loving and accepting ourselves as we are.

- The most important assignment in life is to love unconditionally, beginning with yourself.

- Treat yourself the way you would want others to treat you. If you love and respect yourself, you will love others.
- Be accepting of, and kind to, yourself, for you are stuck with your soul for eternity. Loving yourself as you are is a gift.
- Accept yourself for who you are but constantly strive to evolve into your Higher Self.
- Love yourself. You can only complete your Earthly tasks if you consider yourself worthy of them.
- Witness God's beauty in others and in yourself. Each of us is special to God. We are imperfect beings whom He loves perfectly. Imperfection is perfection.
- Be happy with and within yourself.
- Appreciate and love yourself. Your true self is unique to the cosmos.
- My life-review taught me that before we can let God's light and love in, we must forgive ourselves.
- After my near-death experience, I felt for the first time ever a love and acceptance of myself and others.
- As soon as we believe in our own worth, our soul will be set free.

Chapter 14

Living Fully in the Present Moment

In Chapter 7 it was noted that many of those who crossed to the other side reported in their accounts that Time as we know and experience it on Earth does not exist in the Higher Realms where the past and future do not exist in a linear sense but everything is happening now. Eternity is one second and one second an eternity. On Earth we are used to the concept of linear or sequential time in which we all have a past, a present and a future. But this observation from beyond the veil may indeed be very instructive as an injunction on how we can live our lives more fully in this realm.

Many of us are too busy contemplating and planning our future or pondering over past mistakes or regrets to recognize and appreciate the beauty, wonder and awe of the present moment. Since we cannot undo our past and have only tenuous control over the vagaries and vicissitudes of the future, it is necessary to rejoice in the preciousness and fullness of the present moment. This is all the more so when we acknowledge the absolute impermanence of all things. Our exclusive focus must be an awareness of the present moment – the Eternal Now. Maintaining a constant, clear and focused mind and awareness of what one is doing, thinking and feeling from moment to moment, unencumbered by reflections of our past and anxieties concerning our future, assists us in performing our daily tasks wholeheartedly, meaningfully and mindfully rather than superficially and distractedly.

Such mindfulness penetrates through to the reality of our existence and unmasks worldly appearances and delusions. Through mindfulness we awaken to the appreciation, meaning and joy of our life on Earth. Therefore enjoy to the fullest each fleeting moment of this life as what has passed may well never come again. And let every moment be a new beginning (Zen proverb).

Let us now examine what was imparted in the Higher Realms on living fully in the present moment to those who experienced a near-death experience and shared their story with us.

- Live in the present moment.
- Live in the moment. The future and past are now.
- Live completely in the moment or in the now or in the flow.
- There is no past. There is no future. There is only now.
- Every moment matters. Therefore live mindfully and fully in the present moment.
- Make one second into an eternity and an eternity into a single second.
- Seasons change but make time stand still.
- Do not harbor any expectations for if you do, you are surely bound to be ultimately disappointed. Live each day as fully and preciously as if it was your last.
- Live each day to the fullest as if it was your last.
- Do not be so concerned with planning the future and worrying about the past that you are forgoing the joys of living fully in the present moment.
- Feel the perfection of every moment of your life which has led you to the present moment.
- Death is an exhale which is not followed by an inhale. Reflect on the value of your breath both in sustaining life and in meditative mindfulness of the present moment. Your breath is all that stands between life and physical death. Therefore be conscious of, and in, your breathing.
- Be helpful, present in the moment and a good listener.

Chapter 15

Loving Nature and All Life-Forms

As we shall see shortly, one of the IANDS authors observed in the account of their near-death experience that it was imparted that God is in Nature and that God is Nature.

Elevated or expanded consciousness perceives God/The Creator/Source not only in other human beings but in all sentient beings as well as Nature itself. Everything – all life and the phenomena of Nature – is imbued with spirit and consciousness. All spiritual and physical life and existence are interdependent and connected. God is in Nature (or Mother Earth) as creator, protector and benevolent provider to all sentient beings. Reverence for God and Nature must extend to love and respect for the flora and fauna of this our most beautiful planet as well as gratitude for the Earth's abundant blessings. As it has been said, if we open ourselves to Nature, Nature will open itself to us.

The role of humanity is to be a guardian or steward over Nature, whereby we should act in a manner that is harmonious with Nature rather than act exclusively for the benefit of ourselves. We should therefore not take from Nature more than our reasonable needs require and ensure that we exploit the resources thereof only on a sustainable basis. The natural environment provides life, sustenance and nurture; connection and context; foundation and orientation. We should therefore work with Nature, not against it.

Many IANDS written accounts surveyed offer up some remarkable observations concerning humanity's connection with Nature or Mother Earth and the various flora and fauna thereof, as well as describing Nature's Earth counterpart in Heaven (refer back to Chapter 3 for accounts of the physical description of the Heavenly landscapes). According to the IANDS accounts, Earth is our mother, a living organism, and that humanity can learn much from Nature. The universal laws require us to live in harmony with and respect Nature and not to take therefrom more than our needs require and what can sustainably be produced. From beyond the veil it has also been disclosed that all living sentient creatures and their systems are connected. That humanity's dominionship over them is to steward and care for them, not to abuse or exploit them, and that all life should be respected as precious and sacred. That we should rejoice in the beauty of all life and that consciousness extends to trees, plants and animals (which has already been known by indigenous cultures for thousands of years).

As we observed in Chapter 3, the beautiful landscapes of Heaven are depicted very much like their pristine counterparts on Earth, including beautiful and stately trees which seem alive, gently rolling verdant green hills, streams and ponds, birds and all sorts of other animals. A number of IANDS authors also recounted vividly seeing their childhood pets in Heaven.

Here is what the IANDS authors reported having learned about Nature/Mother Earth and humanity's connection with the animal world.

- God is in Nature; God is Nature. God is everywhere and within us.
- Love Nature, study it closely, learn from it and become one with it.
- Love Nature and sanctify all life.
- Behold and rejoice in the beauty of all life-forms, as they are all created by God. Like us, they have fear and struggle to survive. So have compassion towards them.
- Tune in to Nature and the nature of things.
- Live in harmony with, and deep respect of, Nature.

- Every living sentient creature is one. They must not be harmed. Humanity's dominion over them is to care for, and not exploit or abuse, them.
- Respect all life, including your own. Do not do any harm or injury.
- Your life on Earth is precious. All life is precious.
- You are not less than or greater than any other living sentient being in the world.
- Trees, plants and animals also have consciousness.
- The trees seemed almost alive in a way. It was like they were conscious and communicating with me, like they were happy that I could see them in their true form.
- As a result of my near-death experience, I could feel some radiant energy flowing all around me, especially from the trees, which appeared bright and dark green. I could feel that I was connected to a mysterious source of energy which was all around me.
- I felt one with Nature – the woods, the fields and our neighbor's livestock. I felt "one" with them all. I "heard" them talk to me and I "talked" right back: a telepathy. Even the trees and blades of grass spoke to me. "See how beautiful and perfect we are. All we have to do is grow and exist and BE. We are all 'one.'"
- All created Beings – flora and fauna – know they were created by the Source.
- Animals have souls. Have respect and appreciation for them.
- Animals have souls and reincarnate.
- Our pets offer us companionship and the opportunity to develop love and compassion for all living beings.
- God's creatures are put on Earth to teach us love, compassion and respect. If we cannot love and respect God's creatures, then how can we love one another and God?

- Our pets are reunited with us in Heaven.
- Our pets go to Heaven.
- I saw my childhood dogs in Heaven.
- I saw my childhood dog running in the grass beside me in Heaven.
- Spiritual beings of higher vibration than humans live on Earth as caretakers of its physical life and of the balance of Nature.
- The Earth is our mother, a living organism.
- The planet we call Earth has a proper universal name called Gaia which has its own energy and abundance. Humans manipulate Gaia's energy through their choices. The universal laws require us to live in harmony with Gaia's energy and not to take from Nature more than our needs require and what Gaia can sustainably produce.
- Exchange and share love, compassion, energy and light with Gaia which is also a living entity.
- As a result of my near-death experience, I was less guided by my previous strict religious convictions and more influenced by pantheism.

Chapter 16

The Universal Laws of Attraction and Cause and Effect (Karma)

Some of the IANDS near-death experience accounts include references to so-called universal laws, particularly the Law of Attraction and the Law of Cause and Effect. These laws operate in the Higher Realms as well as the Earthly plane but in a context and conceptual framework different from what we are used to on Earth.

The Universal Law of Cause and Effect or Karma essentially postulates, to borrow from a Biblical metaphor, that what we sow is what we reap. All that we send forth into the Universe is sooner or later returned to us. A wise action will produce good results; an ignorant action will produce negative and harmful consequences. It is a universal or natural law of cause and effect and of action and reaction. Every volitional act produces effects or results. The effects and consequences of our acts ripple outwards to eternity. It is not so much a system of reward or punishment or retributive justice but operates in virtue of its own nature as a universal law. In other words, it is what it is.

The Universal Law of Attraction essentially postulates that like understands and attracts like, and that it manifests or creates the things we are thinking of. We create or manifest not only with our acts but with our thoughts and words. What we think and speak about and the manner in which it is done draws similar energy to us. Positive thoughts and words attract positive energy unto you; negative thoughts and words attract negative energy unto you. We become what we think and speak of. We create for ourselves what we focus on. What we think and speak about, we bring about. In other words, our thoughts and words create our own reality or experience or universe (as well as our delusions and projections). We must take care in what we think and say as thoughts and words create our Earthly reality and experience and can, of course, harm others. What our soul's energy emits draws similar energy back to us, for good or for bad. Therefore, long for and focus on God/Source and the Higher Realms and your soul will be drawn there.

The Law of Attraction:

- Energy flows where your attention goes.
- Like attracts like. Positive attracts positive; negative attracts negative.
- If you are negative and suffering, others absorb it; if you are loving and positive, others absorb it.
- What we think about, we bring about. What we focus on, we will get.
- Your thoughts and your feelings create your life and your own reality.
- Your thoughts instantly create your reality.
- Cleanse your thought process. Thoughts are very powerful; and as you think, so you are. They have creative effects in this world and in the Universe.
- Anything we focus on, we create.
- Focus on what you want rather than on what you do not want. What our mind focuses upon, we will receive.
- When you focus on what you do not have in your life, you will attract more of what you do not have into your life.
- We become what we think about.
- You attract to yourself whatever the thoughts you have inside you.
- Worry and fear attract just that into your life.
- If you emit fear and anger, such emotions will be attracted back to you.
- Everything we experience in life we are attracting into

it. We become what we think about most. Our thoughts manifest or become things and have their own frequency and energy.

- Open yourself up to the abundance of the Universe and you will attract it into your life. There is more than enough to satisfy all.
- Do not strive for the outer things; strive first for the inner things and you will enjoy abundance and wealth in all areas.
- Like understands like. To understand and relate to any of the higher realms or dimensions, you must open up your soul to that particular realm or dimension.

The Law of Cause and Effect (Karma):

- All that we send out comes back to us.
- What we put out into the Universe returns to us.
- What you create is yours.
- The things we do on Earth do matter. The consequences and effects of words, acts and non-action ripple through an eternity.
- As you sow, you reap. Sow love and it shall be returned manifold although you do not intend or expect it. The more we sow on Earth, the more we will reap in Heaven.
- My near-death experience taught me that we reap what we sow and that no purpose in life is too small or insignificant in God's eyes.
- There are karmic reasons for both the good and the bad in our lives.
- Souls are reincarnated. The soul's past lives and fears and unresolved problems accumulated therein may be affecting its current Earthly existence.
- Cause and effect do exist in the higher realms but outside of our Earthly conception of them.

Chapter 17

Positive and Negative Energy

The Universe and everything in it are energy which cannot be created or destroyed and which has always been, and always will be, moving in and through different forms and ever in transition. This is a Universal Law. God/Source is universal energy flowing through everything and making everything one. Universal energy is infinite and so can never be exhausted. Everything is made from the same vibrating universal energy which animates, connects and binds all things together. Everything is created from the same subatomic particles connected to Source energy. Quantum physics confirms that nothing is truly solid; everything is energy. Everything consists of energy waves, and in reality there is nothing solid.

Universal energy emanates from everything, including humans, animals, plants and trees. All living sentient beings are surrounded by their own energy auras which are sometimes visible to the human eye (but clearly perceptible with the so-called "third eye"). Energy intensity and vibrations vary between spiritual and physical matter (with the latter being lower). We are not our Earthly body; we are the energy that is one with that of God/Source. Upon physical death of the body, the energy merely changes form and the soul-consciousness experiences higher vibrations.

Everything exists in a continuous balance between positive and negative or what the Abrahamic religions (Judaism, Christianity and Islam) would term good and evil or what Buddhism and Jainism would refer to as wisdom or enlightenment/awakening and ignorance or unskillfulness. Each soul manifests both positive and negative energy. Energy finds its own equilibrium in the sense that positive energy attracts positive energy; negative energy attracts negative energy (see the previous chapter concerning the Law of Attraction).

Positive energy comprises many of those qualities which mainstream religions attribute as Divine virtues. This includes first and foremost pure and unconditional love that transcends and persists regardless of circumstances. The love and light of God/Source are vibrational energies which flow through and connect all things. Other powerful positive energies include gratitude and thankfulness (high-frequency energies), understanding, acceptance (of others and their flaws) and forgiveness. While this listing is by no means intended to be exhaustive, other notable positive energies include joy, harmony, peace and calmness, kindness, empathy, heartfelt compassion, sensitivity, the radiating outwards of positive thoughts and feelings towards others, serving and caring for others (without expecting anything in return), working towards the highest good of all and surrender to God/Source.

Negative energy is not of God and does not exist in the Higher Realms. As one IANDS author observes, God is not about fear, condemnation or judgment. Humanity and religion have used God to facilitate human control and to instill fear of judgment and condemnation into humans and to shape human belief. Negative thoughts and emotions and substance abuse alter our soul's energy in the Earthly plane. As we have already seen, like attracts like and the manifestation of negative thoughts and deeds will surely be returned to us by the Universe. The killing or harming of other beings is self-harm. Being judgmental, biased and discriminatory towards others also lessens our energy flow and harms our soul. Anger, greed, selfishness, guilt, worry and anxiety are other types of negative energy which alter our soul's energy intensity and vibrations. Illnesses and diseases begin on an energetic level before they manifest physically and are produced by fear. Only the universal energy of unconditional love can eradicate fear and thereby heal the body.

Life is a precious gift from God/Source which should not be prematurely terminated. It is exclusively the Divine prerogative to end life. Killing ourselves and others interferes with and frustrates God's purpose for those lives. Those who have undergone a near-death experience after having unsuccessfully attempted to end their own life report that this is against the universal laws, as we should not attempt to release ourselves from our soul agreement prematurely, having left our life's mission and purpose unfilled.

What follows are the observations noted in the accounts of various IANDS authors classified into three sections: the nature of universal energy; positive energy; negative energy.

The Nature of Universal Energy:

- Energy binds and connects all things together.
- Vibrating energy abounds through the universe, animating and connecting all things.
- Everything is made from the same energy.
- Nothing is solid; everything is energy.
- All life, both seen and unseen, is energy.
- I was told by the Being of Light that there are more energy forms in the Universe than hairs on my head and that the Universe is filled with life and sounds. I was informed that we are made up of tonal frequencies and that we all vibrate to a different sound spectrum.
- The Universe and everything in it are energy which cannot be created or destroyed and which always has been, and always will be, moving in and through different forms and ever in transition.
- Everything is created from the same subatomic particles connected to the Source energy. These particles can change with the determination of the energy that makes up everything.

- The Light and Unconditional Love are the same energy but vibrate at slightly different rates.
- Divine energy is like a warm and embracing electrical current.
- Energy is never lost.
- Energy is not created or destroyed; it merely changes forms. It is a universal law.
- Energies of different dimensions and realms react with each other.
- We are not our physical earthly body; we are the life-force or energy that is one with that of God.
- Energy emanates from everything, including humans, animals, plants and trees.
- All living beings have energy auras around them of different levels and colors. The more brilliant the color, the higher the vibration. A soul's vibration is lower in incarnate physical form. A human therefore cannot see life-forms which spirits of higher vibration can.
- Energy intensity varies; physical bodies have less energy while soul spirits have more energy and higher vibrations.
- I found myself being bathed in shimmering and beautiful warm colors. They seemed to pass right through me into the core of my being. The colors seemed to be causing a strange but wonderful vibrating sensation throughout my body, each hue carrying its own distinct vibration. I had never felt more alive and energetic. I could feel the colors.
- I suddenly found myself in a waiting area, a room with no dimensions but filled with a beautiful light that appeared to have no source. I knew immediately that I was in a place that I knew from before. It was like going home. I remember the vibration was at a much higher rate and I felt completely free. ... When I returned to my body, I felt the painful gravity and the slowdown of the vibration which the earthly plane has to offer.

- My near-death experience filled me with some unknown and overpowering energy.
- Everything exists in a continual balance between light and darkness; positive and negative.
- Positive energy attracts positive energy; negative energy attracts negative energy. Therefore, let your mind be a magnet for the former.
- Light and vibrations heal the soul and the physical body.
- We do not die; our energy merely changes form.
- Upon leaving the human body, the soul experiences a higher vibrational state.

Positive Energy:

- I could feel a magnetic pull and was being pulled into a white light. I wanted to get there as quickly as possible, because of all of these wonderful, ecstatic feelings emanating from the light: unconditional love, forgiveness, empathy, acceptance and deep understanding.
- Create joy for yourselves and others. You are meant to have and deserve happiness.
- Experience joy, peace and calmness.
- Feel love, joy and gratitude to attract positive energy into your life.
- Generate harmony and happiness.
- We need to love one another for peace and harmony to be experienced on Earth.
- Love is the ultimate answer to everything.
- The Light told me to manifest Love, to live Love and to be Love.
- Live a life of love and not of fear.
- The most profound aspect of my near-death experience was that of being completely enveloped in Divine Love and being totally free of fear.

- We must love the unlovable. We must see others and their struggles through the eyes of God. Empathy begets compassion.
- Love one another and accept others' flaws, and ponder their true potential.
- I was told by the Light to connect with others in a positive way, to look for the good in them and to live by the "golden rule."
- Unconditional love is a very, very powerful energy in itself.
- The highest and purest form of Love is unconditional, radiating to all things living, unseen and inanimate.
- Love is the foundational core of everything that exists. Pure love is unconditional. It is not jealous or selfish and does not attach conditions to its flow.
- I experienced a profound sense of love; it is everything. The love was so intense that words defy description.
- Unconditional love is perfect love.
- Unconditional love is a love for all that is, a love that does not differentiate and a love that exists everywhere, including within us.
- Unconditional love is universal and sublime.
- In answer to my question "What is Beyond the Light?", the answer instantaneously formed in my consciousness that there are no limits or boundaries; Love is infinite.
- Unconditional love heals.
- Giving unconditional love is a blessing and returns to the giver an abundance of even more to give.
- Once you experience unconditional love, you shall crave for nothing else. It is the most powerful force in the Universe created by God.
- Love is the most creative powerful force in existence.
- Love is a vibrational energy flowing through and connecting all things like an electrical current.

- Love is warm energy which penetrates the soul and heart.
- Manifest love and compassion towards every living thing. Feel what they are feeling; manifest empathy.
- Material possessions do not matter; it is all about love for your fellow human beings and for God's creatures. The message I received is to love your neighbor, the needy, the homeless and those who do not know any better.
- Manifest your compassion outwardly to others.
- Feel and see with your heart. Perceive and consider important what is on the inside of a person; not on what is outside.
- The only thing that matters is love. Petty stuff does not matter. What we consider important on Earth is not considered so in the higher realms.
- Be more empathetic and less judgmental.
- Be sensitive to others.
- Become the essence of compassion.
- Consciously evolve your soul by practicing love and kindness to all living beings and live in harmony with yourself and Nature.
- Send out waves of loving-kindness energy.
- Loving-kindness towards others is a manifestation of the Light.
- Be loving and kind in your thoughts, words and deeds. Be motivated by your soul heart.
- It is good to do kind deeds to others, but even more important to radiate positive thoughts and feelings towards them.
- Generate positive and good thoughts and avoid petty distractions.
- Let the Light of God shine in and through you so that you may send loving thoughts and vibrations to others.
- Intend for your thoughts, words and deeds to have a positive effect for the highest good of all.

- If it benefits only yourself, avoid it; if it benefits only those around you, act accordingly. Serve and care for others' material and spiritual needs without expecting anything in return.
- If you make choices that benefit others without intending to have, or expecting, anything back from them, your soul will feel love, kindness and positivity.
- Let love and light be your essence.
- Wisdom and compassion walk hand-in-hand with each other.
- Empathize with the thoughts and feelings and circumstances of others.
- Love everything and become one with it.
- Profoundly love all people without distinction and focus on the good in them. Put others first.
- Be exceedingly thankful for the countless blessings God has conferred upon you. Joy and gratitude are two of the highest vibrational states.
- Be grateful for your life, soul, breath and all that sustains you.
- Be grateful for your Earthly life and respect it.
- There is so much to be grateful for and joyful about if we set aside the time to reflect thereon.
- Be grateful for the things you have rather than complain about what you don't have. When you focus on what you don't have, you will attract more of what you don't have into your life. Focus on what brings you joy and gratitude.
- Acceptance and forgiveness are the keys to Heaven.
- Accept others as they are rather than how we think they should be.
- Accept the unacceptable and thereby embrace peace and calm.
- Give up. Let go. Stop fighting. Accept. Surrender.
- Surrender yourself completely to God.

- It is all about forgiveness.
- Forgiveness may be one of the most difficult things for us to do, but it is one of the greatest and noblest things we can ever do.
- Forgiveness heals the soul.
- Forgiveness is the best gift that we can give to ourselves. Lack of forgiveness poisons those who refuse to "let it go," and continues to affect our lives in a negative way until we do forgive. Forgiveness sets us free. If we choose to hang on to the hurts and resentments, we sentence ourselves to an existence based on fear not only in this life, but also in the next life you are given, and the next, until we learn. What matters is that we choose to free ourselves from the bondage that goes with the lack of forgiveness, lack of love, lack of mercy or lack of compassion.
- Before we can let God's love in, we must forgive ourselves.
- When your heart sincerely asks for forgiveness, you shall be forgiven.
- There is good and evil in each soul. Face towards the Light and turn your back on the darkness. The darkness cannot comprehend the Light.
- Embrace righteousness and abhor evil.
- Become the best version of yourself.
- For relationships to be healthy, complain not of the faults of the other, but focus on their good and positive qualities. Appreciate and acknowledge their strengths and relational impediments will fall away.

Negative Energy:

- According to universal laws, Earthly existence is based on duality. When negativity no longer exists, one is no longer a resident of this planet as it presently works. Our mission is to acknowledge the existence of this duality and then to prevent negativity from impeding our individual paths by embracing the need for more positivity in our lives. This is the epitome of our life lesson and the beginning of unconditional love and harmony with all life.

- Negative energy held and manifested by humans is a product of their lower level of enlightenment.
- Negative energy is incompatible with love and acceptance and therefore does not exist in the higher realms.
- I understood that we must release the density (negative energy) within us that holds back unconditional love and prevents the Light from flowing through us.
- Do not kill or harm other sentient beings as you are also harming yourself. Your life-review will surely cause you to empathetically feel personally the harm you have caused to others.
- I was told that there would be no judgment or penalty for having taken my own life. My deed of self-destruction was forgiven. However, the Being of Light told me that I had no right to take my life, or any life for that matter. Only God has authority to give and take a life. Life is sacred and to be cherished. We are all loved unconditionally by the Creator.
- I learned that we must not attempt our self-destruction for to do so is committing the ultimate crime against oneself, against the purpose of this life and against the wisdom of God. God is our Creator but we have been given the power of choice (through Free Will) to shape our own life and final destiny. As soon as I believed in my own worth and my responsibility to life and to all those around me, my soul was set free.
- We harm ourselves when we hurt others. We harm ourselves when we make poor choices which do not serve our highest good and the highest good of all souls around us.

- Fear does not exist in the Divine realms; it is an instrument of earthly control.
- There is no reason to worry, no reason to fear. Everything happens for a reason and is unfolding as it should.
- Do not fear or grieve for what you have left behind.
- Fear and guilt over things which have gone wrong in our lives are not necessarily justified, as they may be part of our life's learning journey.
- Worry and guilt are negative emotions and energy.
- Worry and fear attract just that into your life.
- Have no fear and no judgment.
- Judging others is human folly confined to the earthly realm.
- If we condemn others, we condemn a part of ourselves. Never judge another, but try to understand and empathize.
- To judge others is placing a condition on otherwise Unconditional Love and on life itself.
- One should avoid bias and the temptation to judge others.
- Do not be afraid.
- Have no fear.
- Being judgmental stops the flow of energy and light and produces denser vibrations.
- Do not feel obliged to lower your vibrations in order to fit in with the ways of the world. To do so will impede your soul's evolutionary progress.
- Do not live your life consumed with self (your own ego) and thereby hurt and let down others.
- Our negative thoughts and substance abuse can alter human energy. If you emit fear and anger, such emotions will be attracted back to you. Like attracts like.
- Focus on the intent of other people. If their intent is self-focused or negative towards others or disturbs the harmony of Nature and the Universe, it is best to avoid them.

- Each of us has an aura which is the energy field around us. Disease of the body can first be detected in the aura before it manifests in bodily form.
- Illnesses and diseases start on an energetic level before they manifest physically.
- Sound can heal bodily ailments and diseases. Color, sound frequencies and music bring forth healing.

Chapter 18

Our Physical Body, Its Limitations and Eventual Demise

What is our physical body and its relationship to us and our life?

We are not merely our bodies. Our bodies contain our soul-consciousness or life-force which, as we have seen in Chapter 5, is eternal. The physical body itself is perishable and has been described in *The Tibetan Book of the Dead: The Main Verses of the Six Bardos* as a compound of flesh and blood which is nothing more than "a transitory illusion." However, our body is much more than that and has been described in the Christian *New Testament* as "a temple of the Holy Spirit within you" (1 Corinthians chapter 6 verse 19). It is a temple of the Divine spark that dwells in each of us.

The authors of various IANDS near-death experience accounts utilize a variety of descriptions of the function of our physical body. The body has been described, for example, as the soul's prison for the duration of our Earthly lifetime. It has also been described as the soul's shell or shelter or its temporary home or resting-place. Others describe the body as an Earthly vessel which is borrowed temporarily to enable our soul-consciousness to experience Earthly life and to learn and grow from that experience. As the body is a temple for the Divine, it should be well cared for, maintained and respected, and not subjected to excesses.

Our physical bodies are such that we are by nature subject to various limitations and restrictions during our Earthly sojourn. We are indeed confined in the Earthly plane to verbal communication and to spatial and temporal constraints. Most of us cannot detect higher vibrational spiritual realms of consciousness. Our experiences in the Earthly realm are not as sharp, vivid and expansive (compared with the Higher Realms) due to lower vibrations. Human existence tends to be heavy, dense, slow and limited compared with increased vibrations, expanded awareness, perception and consciousness, and freedom of movement experienced in the Higher Realms (see Chapter 7 on "Higher Spiritual Realms").

Our physical body and Earthly identity are temporarily borrowed to allow us to play our transient cameo role in the play called Life. Upon completion of the play (the death of our body), they are no longer required. What, then, is the significance of the death of our physical body?

Many fear death and are so preoccupied with the prospect of death that they fail to remain in the moment and live their life to the fullest. But as the NDE accounts tell us, although death is the extinction of our body, our soul-consciousness is eternal and continues on lifetime after lifetime. There is no reason then to fear the death of our body. In fact, many of the NDE accounts essentially observe that rather than something to fear, death of the body is something to look forward to. In reality, death is an illusion.

The death of our body has been beautifully and elegantly described in some of the IANDS accounts. Basically it is the separation or disconnection of the soul-consciousness from the body. Upon death, it is said that we leave behind our physical pain and our Earthly cares and anxieties. Death is a shedding of our physical existence and a transition of our soul-consciousness to a spiritually-based experiential existence in which our energy assumes a new form and our soul transitions to heightened and more acute thought, perception, awareness and consciousness. Our death in the physical Earthly plane re-births us into the spiritual realms which have been described by some of the authors as the Ultimate Reality in which the true nature of all things may be more readily recognized. Our births in the physical and spiritual realms have indeed been described by one author as sacred events. The death of our body is the leaving behind of our temporary home and a return to our real or true home for rest, self-assessment and debriefing. It is a natural continuation of an eternal process of our spiritual evolution towards God/Source.

What follows are various observations and descriptions made by the IANDS authors concerning the nature of our physical body and its limitations as well as the spiritual significance of its death.

The Nature of the Physical Body and Its Limitations:

- Your body is an earthly vessel which you are temporarily borrowing. Therefore respect and treat it well.
- You are much more than your physical body.
- Our physical body is but a shell or house to contain our soul during its Earthly journey.
- I do not say "body" any longer; I say "lifeshell."
- I understood that my body was my shell for my time on this earth.
- Our body and spirit are one. The body is the soul's container or receptacle. Our body entraps our soul in the earthly plane.
- The body is the soul's prison – the soul a passenger on a raft (body) on an ocean of Earthly life.
- Our human body is connected to higher vibrational levels. It is dense, heavy and limiting.
- The physical body is a vessel that enables our higher consciousness to inhabit it in order to learn and grow from our Earthly experiences.
- Your physical body and Earthly name are temporarily borrowed so that you may play your role in this transient play called Life. Upon completion of our role, we leave both behind.

- Most spirits of human physical form cannot detect higher vibrational spiritual realms of consciousness.
- Our Earthly life is like a caterpillar. In human form, we are limited and move slowly with our cumbersome bodies. On death, we shed the chrysalis (transitional state) and take on a more beautiful form like a butterfly.

Death of the Physical Body:

- Do not fear death as it is illusory.
- Life does not end when we die.
- Death is not the end, but only the beginning of something more glorious than we can ever imagine.
- Death is not a finality; rather, it is a transition from one realm or state to another.
- Our souls never die.
- When our body dies, our soul-consciousness does not die.
- Dying is a natural part of life and continuing consciousness.
- Fear of death is human error. Our souls are eternal and thus continue on.
- There is no need to fear physical death as your consciousness survives it. Your death in the physical realm re-births you into the spiritual realm.
- People fear death, like a thief in the night no one can avoid. I know this to be farthest from the truth. Within death, there is a complete cleansing of the spirit, a washing away of our realities of the flesh and an awakening of the spirit to truths no language can begin to describe. Death is a beginning, not a destination.
- I no longer fear death as I know now from my (out-of-body) experience that my soul survives my bodily death.
- I used to have a great fear of death and dying but not anymore.

- Death is a shedding of our physical/material existence for a spiritually-based existence.
- The death of the physical body is our spirit shedding its earthly skin.
- Death is the soul's transition of experiential existences to other planes or realms.
- Physical death is birth into the Ultimate Reality of the spiritual world which is more real than the earthly realm.
- Having shed my physical body, I felt more real than ever before. I learned how it feels to truly be alive as opposed to just existing.
- While outside my body, I never thought of myself as being "dead"; in fact, I felt more alive than ever. I was acutely aware of the Divine Presence, the Creator and spirit guides all around me.
- Death is painless. It is like going to sleep but you are still awake and alert. We are more alive after the death of our body than we are in this earthly plane.
- While the process leading up to the death of the body may involve pain and suffering, the moment of death, in which we surrender to the call to return to our real home, is painless. Our soul simply transitions to a new and different realm.
- Physical death is not the end but a change or transition or a movement forward. We come from "the other side" and return there when we shed our physical body. Our energy assumes a new form.
- Death is like being extricated from a tight confined space. It is a leaving behind of heaviness, density and slowness. The soul's vibrations increase, allowing it an expanded consciousness, freedom of movement and experience of Love.
- What humans refer to as physical death is one of the Creator's greatest gifts, used for the transition of your spirit into higher realms.

- Death is a process of continuing our spiritual evolutionary journey. Our births into the earthly realm and our births into the spiritual realm are sacred events.
- Physical death is a natural continuum of the soul's eternal transitioning journey.
- Death is a transition to a higher state of consciousness.
- There is no such thing as death; demise of the physical body is merely an escape or release therefrom for the soul and its transition to a higher state of consciousness.
- Physical death is a doorway to Home.
- The other side of the veil is our true home. Death is not the end but only a transition to our true home.
- Death is returning home, an awakening or heightened awareness.
- Death is a returning Home for debriefing and reprogramming.
- Death is the separation of the soul from the physical body. It is a release from its Earthly prison.
- When you discard your body, you discard your pain and earthly cares.
- My soul left my body through my head. I saw my own body in front of me, lying on the bed. Marvelous, immeasurable joy inundated my being. I felt no pain, no sorrows, nothing but wellness and delight as I had never experienced before.
- Upon leaving my body, I felt weightless, not just in the physical sense, but also in an emotional sense. I was aware that I was no longer in the emotional pain that had overtaken my life. I was in such a state of peace. I experienced newfound freedom.
- When you die, the pain is leaving. There is no pain in leaving the body.
- There is no longer any pain when you leave the physical body.

- On death our soul disconnects from our physical body and no longer suffers pain and anguish.
- The part that is TRULY me had left my body and was in a place of pure light – a warm, gentle, loving fog had enveloped me and was me. All of my pain and trauma disappeared. I was welcomed by three Beings of Light with the most incredible love, acceptance and compassion.
- When your soul leaves your body, you become detached from the earthly realm and become an emotionally neutral and distant observer of events therein.
- I was not at all worried about the fact that I was dead. Knowing that I had died seemed totally irrelevant and unimportant. I was not even slightly curious or interested in the body I had left behind.
- Once you cross over the veil, you cannot return to the earthly plane, at least in a way you would remember or recount. If the body is too weak and frail and ravaged by disease or it has received catastrophic accident-related injuries, the soul cannot return to the body and must cross over.
- Each of us dies at the right moment. It may not seem so in the Earthly realm but it is so in the spiritual realms.
- By accepting the inevitability and purpose of one's physical death, we become serene and peaceful.

Chapter 19

Our Spiritual Re-Birth and Life-Review

As we have seen in the previous chapter, our physical death is our re-birth into the spiritual realm; re-birth in the sense that we have already experienced countless lifetimes, births and deaths in our soul's evolutionary journey. As part of that journey, many IANDS authors who recount their out-of-body experience refer to undergoing what some term a "life-review" in which the soul is shown a replay of the life they have just lived and invited to reflect essentially on what they learned from their life experiences, whether they practiced unconditional love and how they might have acted better towards others. This is important as what lies ahead for us on our soul's evolutionary journey depends on how we lived, and learned from, our most recent incarnation.

Describing the nature of the life-review may be divided into the substance of what it is all about and the process in which it is undertaken. In relation to substance, the purpose of the life-review is basically a stock-take or "exit interview" for the edification and evolution of our soul-consciousness. How could we have done better with our time on Earth in that particular incarnation? The Beings of Light typically ask questions such as these when the soul is watching a replay of their entire life including their thoughts, words and deeds, both positive and negative, and their interactions and experiences with other living beings:

- What have you done with your life?
- What did you learn and what Divine knowledge did you acquire?
- Did you understand what unconditional love is and did you practice it?

- How did you love, help and care for others?
- Did you create joy?
- What have you done that was completely selfless in the sense of not being motivated by personal gain?

According to the IANDS authors, we are shown those occasions when we manifested love to others and those occasions when we hurt others to such a degree that they doubted their self-worth or were diminished in their own capacity to manifest love and be loved. Through insensitivity, did we hurt others and how could we have acted differently to secure the highest outcome for all concerned? We are invited to reflect on these matters, to acknowledge our "mistakes" and to learn therefrom. One's conduct is not so much wrong or mistaken but rather not helpful to the soul's development and that of the other souls affected.

Souls learn through the life-review that what we consider important in the Earthly plane – power, wealth and fame – mean nothing in the Higher Realms; conversely, what we consider relatively insignificant in the Earthly realm – like feeding a stray cat or extending a small kindness to a stranger – may be the most profound and meaningful. Souls are also taught that we should never underestimate how impactful our thoughts, words and deeds are on others and their unforeseen and extended consequences. Some IANDS authors use the metaphor of dropping a pebble into the middle of a still pond or pushing a domino which then cascades forward taking down many other dominos in quick succession. The choices we make through the exercise of our Free Will (see Chapter 12) and our thoughts, words and deeds are indeed powerful and influential, and have lasting effects on countless others as they ripple outwards or cascade forward. It is truly the Universal Law of Cause and Effect at work (see Chapter 16).

But a most important point concerning the life-review is that it is educational rather than condemnatory in nature. It is a journey of self-realization. The only "judgment" which is made on how we lived our life is made by us. We are invited to reflect on our acts and our omissions – things not said or done (which should have been said or done) in a clear and undistorted light. How could the best and highest outcome for us and those around us have been achieved? There is, of course, nothing to stop us from engaging in a "preemptive" or anticipatory life-review right now to enable us to better prepare for what may well lie ahead of us on our soul's evolutionary journey.

Concerning the process of a life-review, it typically involves what has been described as a holographic 3-D movie; a panoramic virtually instantaneous review of life's most significant moments. It involves a fast-moving display of visual images and associated feelings and emotions clearly and vividly presented. In one case, it was described as one's life flashing before them like flipping pages of a book. But your soul is much more than a passive observer during the process. The soul witnesses their life from a variety of different perspectives: from a third party objective observer's point of view, from the soul's point of view and from the perspective of those who were affected by the soul's acts and deeds in positive and negative ways. The soul experiences the thoughts, feelings and emotions of those who were affected by the soul's positive and negative conduct, thereby transcending the soul's own selfish perspective while acquiring the perspective of those who were affected by the soul's conduct and choices. The soul feels respectively the happiness, joy, pain, anger and hurt of those who the soul was kind and insensitive to. It is the ultimate exercise in empathy – being in the shoes, so to speak, of others and feeling the intended and unintended effects of the soul's acts and omissions during its Earthly lifetime.

As one IANDS author observes, each soul has a record of every thought, word spoken and act done which forms the basis of the life-review (reminiscent of the so-called Akashic Records).

Dr. Eben Alexander, author of *Proof of Heaven: A Neurosurgeon's Journey into the Afterlife* in which he recounts the experiences of his own near-death experience, states that his own NDE convinced him that "there is a secret part of ourselves that is recording every last aspect of our earthly lives, and that this recording process commences at the very, very beginning."

What follows are various observations of IANDS authors describing their particular life-review experience and what they learned about its purpose and significance.

- Acknowledge your mistakes to learn and grow.
- You are the victim and beneficiary of all your actions.
- My life-review imparted to me that through our mistakes, we learn.
- I was told that our earthly actions and even our thoughts mean a great deal more than we can ever imagine.
- I could see every part of my life, every event all at once. Although it seemed instantaneous, I knew that every moment was there. My hard drive was downloaded, as it were, and my life was replayed in fast-forward.
- I learned from my life-review that it is not about judgment but rather self-realization and a step in the evolution of the soul in relation to understanding unconditional love and acquiring Divine knowledge.
- The love you give is yours for all eternity; you only answer for your incompletions – all the things not said or done. You observe all the paths not taken in life but which might have been taken.
- My life-review was all about what works and what doesn't work. How could I have acted differently to create a more positive outcome overall to elevate my soul?
- During my life-review, the Being of Light asked me in a nonverbal manner whether I had loved and how did I treat others.

- During my life-review, I was asked: "What have you done with your life?"
- I was asked: "What have you done with your life? To what extent did you learn to love and assist others? What knowledge did you acquire? Did you do selfish acts or selfless acts?" The process was educational rather than condemnatory in nature. My life-review comprised a series of fast-moving pictures akin to slides, clearly and vividly presented.
- The Being of Light asked me what had I done with my life and what I had learned. There was no accusation or condemnation. The soul is invited to reflect on their recent life and encouraged to follow the best pathway.
- A spiritual Being of Light presents the soul with a review of its life to solicit reflection and learning therefrom. It is very rapid, almost instantaneous, similar to a motion picture. A display of visual images and associated feelings and emotions is experienced by the soul.
- I was asked during my life-review what I had ever done in my life that was totally selfless? What kind words or deeds were spoken or done that were not motivated by the prospect of personal gain?
- The Being of Light asked me: "What actuated you? Did you act out of righteousness or because it was good for you personally?"
- All of us will eventually be asked three questions: "What did you learn on Earth and how did you help others? Did you create joy on Earth?"
- Our life-review also includes things we did not do but which we should have done. It is a stock-take for the edification and development of our soul.
- Our life-review is like an exit interview, seeing our life as we lived it and understanding things differently in a new light and then moving on.

- Each soul has a record of everything thought, spoken and done. This forms part of the soul's Life-Review. Each act of kindness, however small, is recorded.
- I was taken to a vault that held information concerning souls' life cycles and growth.
- I was shown the review of my entire life: every thought, every word, every action I had thought, said and done during my lifetime on Earth. It was complete in the blink of an eye. All was known and understood. I felt no judgment or condemnation; only unconditional acceptance, peace and love.
- Every significant lifetime event is shown to the soul which recalls how it felt at the time and the emotions felt by others.
- During my life-review, I could see and feel how I had hurt people out of my own carelessness.
- Do not underestimate how impactful every thought, word and deed is and how Earth and all of Creation are affected.
- I learned that our actions and words are powerful and possess rippling and lasting consequences. Therefore, we must empathize with others around us who may be affected before we speak and act.
- I felt and experienced the scenes from my life from the perspectives of all those present.
- One's entire life is witnessed from a third party observer's point of view, from the soul's point of view and that of those who were affected by the soul's acts and deeds. The soul feels the feelings and emotions of those who were affected by the soul's positive and negative conduct. The soul gains the perspective of the humans who were affected by the soul's choices. Even the soul's seemingly innocent choices can have implications beyond which we could ever have imagined. It therefore matters deeply

what choices we as humans make in exercise of our gift of free will. One's conduct is not so much wrong but rather not helpful to the soul's development and that of the other souls affected.

- During a review of my life, I remember seeing my sister at 6 years old and myself at 5. In the review, I was very mean and hateful to my sister, calling her names and making her cry. The Light telepathically informed me of my hatred. At that point, I felt overwhelmed with guilt, shame and humiliation. These feelings were very intense and the worst I had ever known. I had never felt anything with that intensity before and I just wanted the review to end, but it was not over and about to get worse. What I felt next was the worst pain I have ever experienced. Suddenly I realized I had become my sister. I was put inside her so that I could now experience the gut-wrenching pain that she felt due to my actions. I was told by the Light that I had to change my ways by loving instead of hating and that we should love all and hate none.

- Our life-review examines those lifetime events when love most manifested itself and those times when we hurt others to such a degree that they doubted their self-worth or felt diminished in their ability to love and be loved.

- There is no judgment during the life-review; only reflection.

- All throughout the life-review process, the only entity which judged me was myself. The Light did not praise or condemn my earthly actions or inactions, but paused some scenes and asked for my observations and reflection.

- Each soul is assisted by spirit guides in a review of the soul's immediate past life. There is no judgment; nor is there any punishment. That God would judge or punish is a human construct as God only loves. Only the soul itself is required to judge, evaluate and reflect as it is its harshest critic.

- My angel told me that I must review my life in order to cleanse my soul, and that it is important that I learn from this. The angel told me that my life is evaluated by the most powerful judge there is – that being me!
- One's entire life, including all of the good and bad deeds, are reflected upon in a clear and undistorted light. One's life cannot be misrepresented or lied about. Nothing can be concealed.
- Every thing said, thought and done from infancy to death is reviewed before the angels and the Heavenly Light.
- During a panoramic, instantaneous review of the most significant events of the life just lived on Earth, a Being of Light poses a nonverbal question or questions and asks the soul to reflect on and evaluate that life.
- A Being of Light told me that she was God's messenger who was assigned to review my life. She had the ability to reach inside my mind and pull out the memories and events of my life, which we reviewed together like a flickering movie.
- Everything I had ever said or done was shown to me. It was like watching a movie reel. God does not judge or condemn us; we judge ourselves.
- There is no condemnation or judgment; only reflection upon how one could have acted differently to secure a better outcome for all concerned.
- Any guilt or remorse you might feel witnessing your life-review is not yours to take or keep.
- A Life-Review is re-living and an opportunity to consider what our soul has learned from the incarnation's experiences and interactions. There is no judgment or condemnation. Only we judge ourselves from a perspective outside ourselves with clear-sighted vision. We discover how profound an impact seemingly insignificant actions had on others and how the exercise of our free will and

decision-making ripples outward to countless others. And the hurt we inflict on others in turn causes them to inflict hurt on yet others that we could never have anticipated.

- My life-review was a 360-degree movie projection displaying the domino or ripple effects of what harsh and unkind words and deeds have on others and which are passed on to yet others. You feel the anger and sadness of your victims.

- A series of images and experiences were displayed like a projector displaying images on a flat screen. I could see, feel, think, hear and experience the emotions, thoughts and experiences of everyone I had either direct or indirect contact with.

- When I realized that I was dead, my life started flashing through my mind like flipping pages through a book. It seemed to finish in a second. Everything I did and everything I didn't do but could have done was reviewed.

- You don't just observe what you did but you feel the repercussions of your actions – the injury, fears, pain and anger of those who suffered at your hands and the ripple effects they in turn passed on to yet others.

- My life-review was like a holographic movie. You are a witness to your own life, an objective observer because you feel the feelings of everyone involved and see each person's point of view rather than your own selfish perspective. Our thoughts, words and deeds are like pebbles dropped in the middle of a pond, sending out ripples to eternity.

- Our actions are like a single drop of water landing in the middle of a pond. It creates ripples which affect not only our immediate interactions but those others with whom they in turn come into contact. The impacts are often unforeseen and never-ending.

- If you can imagine a series of dominos cascading downwards like water down staggered steps, then this was the experience of being in the shoes of other people and experiencing both the intended and unintended effects of my contact with them. I saw a multitude of opportunities to help people and be loving and kind, but I often chose to ignore these opportunities and instead focus on myself.

- My life-review was like watching a movie in which I was the leading actor. You see people who received love from you without you knowing it. You witness the ripple effects of your good deeds. You see all the good deeds done by others because of love you had shown to them. Small kindnesses result in unforeseen but profound manifestations of love.

- My life-review was like watching a holographic 3-D movie. I saw and understood everything that had ever happened to me. I witnessed things I had done, things others had done to me and places I'd been to. I just observed and felt no judgment. I was even shown things and events I had long forgotten.

- It was as if I was watching a very complex hologram that showed the story of my life, where I was the hologram, but also watching from a third person perspective. I felt all the pain, loneliness, fear and suffering that had been part of my life, but all of the love too. Everything I had ever done, ever felt, ever had done to me, I relived. I also felt others' feelings as if they were my own. Every time I had hurt someone I felt their pain as my own. Every time I brought happiness to someone, I felt that as if it were my own. I got to see how these people, in turn, turned around and either spread the good feeling to someone else, or hurt someone with the pain I had given to them. And then I felt their pain. I was overwhelmed. I was shown many different futures all at the same time. I was also shown years ahead, to the end of my Earthly life and beyond.

- I learned during my life-review that power, wealth and fame mean nothing in the higher realms. Sending loving and positive thoughts and vibrations means something.
- What my life-review taught me was that the most extraordinary and significant moments of our lives are not what we consider them to be – wealth, possessions, fame, promotions etc. What we consider to be trivial actions or small kindnesses (like feeding a stray cat) are the most significant.
- Small acts of kindness count for much in the higher spiritual realms.
- Even small acts of kindness can trigger unforeseen positive consequences for others as the effects thereof ripple outwards.
- During my life-review I discovered that many trivial events in my past towards which I harbored resentment or held grudges or remembered being injured were actually very different from the way I had remembered them. I had a clear sense that many of these things not only didn't happen in the way that I remembered them but in fact may well have been due to my shortcomings such as anger, selfishness and greed.
- Placed in front of me to see and feel was my life-review … in color. I had to see and feel all the good I had done (and the good I didn't even know I did). I could actually feel the joy each person felt when I touched their life in a loving way. Reviewing my random acts of kindness gave me the most joy because I was able to feel the difference I had made in someone's life that I hadn't realized at the time … and I didn't even know them. Little acts of kindness mean so much to God. I also had to see and feel all the hurtful things I had done (even the hurtful things I didn't know I did). I had to feel the person's hurt I had caused. God was not judging me; I was judging myself.

I was so ashamed and there was no hiding. God asked me what different choices could and should I have made and what I was learning from my review. This was clearly not the punishing God I had been taught to believe in. Although I was having a hard time forgiving myself, God had already forgiven me. Before we can let God's love in, we must forgive ourselves. God wants us to accept His love for us. Once that was revealed to me, I was able to more openly and honestly look at my life. God loves us the way we love our children. Even when they do something wrong, we still love them. Our love for them does not change.

- I was told that a life-review can include reviews of experiences and existences in other realms of realities and in other worlds.
- Are the things you have created in your life until now worthy of you?
- What lies ahead for us depends on how we have lived and learned from our current existence.
- We all get our day of atonement (at-one-ment) when our physical body dies and our soul meets the Light.
- Why not prepare for your post-physical death life-review by conducting the same during this lifetime?

Chapter 20

Potpourri

The French term *potpourri* denotes, amongst other things, a mixture of unrelated things. During the course of my research into the IANDS near-death experience accounts, I came across numerous observations and exhortations made by the authors in their accounts as a result of what they brought back with them from their out-of-body experience. These concise observations and exhortations concern the importance of an inner spiritual life, the virtues of simplicity and innocence, what really matters and how to live our life on Earth. They do not appear as such to squarely fit within any of the chapter themes presented in this book. Nevertheless, because of their significance in their own right and their potentially profound impact, I have chosen to include them in this chapter.

- Beauty comes of all things.
- My near-death experience was definitely not a dream. I was there! The experience is as fresh in my mind as if it happened yesterday. No mere dream has ever lasted that long.
- I was profoundly changed by my near-death experience. I realized how precious our life on Earth is and how quickly it could be gone.
- Consider each day as a gift and an opportunity.
- Never lose your conscience.
- Listen to your conscience, the gentle whisperings of your higher self and God within.
- Since my near-death experience, I rely on my inner voice more often than I do reason and logic.

- Imperfect is perfect. A perfect God perfectly loves our imperfect souls.
- Nothing can separate us from God.
- The Truth lies within you.
- Do not be frightened about what you do not understand.
- Eternity lies in the spiritual hearts of us all.
- There is no such place as outward, but only inward.
- What we cannot see (the spiritual realms) is as important as that which we can see (the physical or material realms).
- Your vision will always be impaired until you begin to see through the eyes of others.
- All religions are merely vain attempts to express a simple Truth. The Golden Rule (do unto others as you would have them do unto you) is the central rule to live our lives by.
- My near-death experience revealed to me how inaccurately God is perceived, interpreted and understood. Religious zealotry is not of God.
- Beliefs are far less important in the higher spiritual realms.
- Be more spiritual and less religious.
- Having had my near-death experience, I no longer believe in organized religion but I do believe in spirituality.
- As one who has undergone a near-death experience, I do not go to church, yet feel a very deep spiritual connection to God.
- My near-death experience transcended religion. Religion is not required to connect with the Divine.
- The messenger is of less significance than the message that must be absorbed.
- I have not become a believer of any "religion" as a result of my near-death experience. But I have experienced a "shift" in how I view matters of life and death.
- I have dropped all forms of organized religion and find myself open to much more universal truths.

- Love is what is important, not religion.
- My very Catholic outlook on life had been changed by my near-death experience to a more pantheistic one.
- My near-death experience went beyond the boundaries of my religion; a journey I must make alone. I have to look beyond.
- Since my near-death experience, I have reevaluated my religious beliefs and no longer attend church, feeling that it is dogmatic and misinterpreted (corrupted) to others' desires. I believe that energy is the basis of all and is the true answer to all questions.
- Be more spiritual and less materialistic.
- Do not strive for the outer things; strive first for the inner things.
- All spirituality is good. No one belief system is better than the other.
- We are all accepted by God regardless of our specific religious preference.
- Prayer is real; in a state of meditative prayer, you tap into the ultimate power of all that is, was and ever shall be, to change the physical and spiritual manifestation of people and events on Earth.
- Search for the Truth. Your eternity is in your hands. If you ask God, He will save you. But you have to ask. That's called prayer.
- Be simple and childlike.
- Everything that truly matters – love, joy, truth and honesty – are to be found in the smiling eyes and face of an innocent child.
- Look into the eyes of others and see God's love reflected back.
- It is a blessing to approach the end of our life on Earth with the innocence, love, joy and spontaneity of a young child.

- Do not say in words what you do not think and feel in your heart.
- Speak less and listen more.
- We are not who we think we are.
- We never see ourselves as others see us; we only see our mirror reflection.
- We are the living hope of our ancestors.
- Wars and suffering are not created by God, but are created by the human race out of fear, hatred, greed and vainglory.
- Before a catastrophic accident (such as an air disaster or serious motor vehicle accident), our souls peel away from our bodies to avoid experiencing the pain and suffering.
- At the point of impact, I was being hugged safely in the cocoon of God's love. I did not feel the (car) accident at all.
- During the split second prior to the point of impact (of my accident), my mind was somewhere outside my body. I felt no pain and was very relaxed. My whole life flashed before me. I remembered things that had happened to me a long time ago and I remembered every detail. But the most remarkable thing is that I never felt afraid. It was almost as if I were a spectator watching someone else being involved in the accident. Every mistake that I had done in my life, knowingly and unknowingly, flashed before me.
- I became aware that I was outside my body and I remember feeling with surprise and wonder that I had known this feeling before my life had begun, before I was born. I could feel my real self and this was joyous. I was looking down on my life and seeing how unimportant all the hassles were. I could see life as though it were a game I had been playing and how all the moves were just part of the game.

- After my near-death experience, I had an insatiable desire to learn everything about physics and spiritual healing.

- Since my near-death experience, I let nature heal myself and strongly believe in the mind-body connection and a universal God. I developed an amazing ability to heal people.

- Having had a near-death experience, I now quite literally take on the pain of others. I feel their pain with my whole being.

- What changed for me as a result of my near-death experience? I now feel people's emotions as though they are inside me. I now have reliable intuition.

- Following my near-death experience, a doorway to the spirit world opened up to me.

- My near-death experience has made my life rich by unselfishness and becoming more detached from earthly matters. I no longer have fear of anything, including death.

- After my near-death experience, I am attuned to healing energies and intuitively feel the feelings of others. It is not so much about what I have achieved or can achieve in my life but more about seeking to understand what and who I truly am.

- After my near-death experience, colors seemed brighter and detail was sharper. Other lights had colors around them like a spectrum and people sometimes had auras of color around them.

- As a result of my near-death experience, I feel like I have a piece of Heaven in my heart now, and that it is opening like a flower.

- I cannot describe in words no matter how hard I try the beauty, completeness and overwhelmingness of my near-death experience and how life-changing it was, and the loneliness of it sometimes, as many do not believe in what happened to me or find it difficult to relate to what I describe.

- I knew – with total certainty – that everything was evolving exactly the way it should and that the ultimate destiny of every living being is to return to the Source, the Light, Pure Love.
- Those of us who have undergone a near-death experience have been called back to their Earthly life to teach and share their experiences and knowledge with others. We are to honor a special mission to help humanity realize that there is indeed no death. We simply "move on" and continue to evolve in our journey back towards the Light.
- Life on Earth pales in comparison to what awaits us.

Chapter 21

Conclusion

We lead busy and rather complicated lives and our attention is often diverted away from deep metaphysical and philosophical questions by the amusements and distractions of the world. Nevertheless, at least at one point in our lives, most of us have pondered some, if not all, of these questions: What happens when we die? Is there an afterlife? Does God exist? Is there a Heaven? Do each of us have a soul or consciousness that survives the death of our physical body? What is the purpose of our Earthly existence and what is our mission here? Are we judged on a reward-punishment basis or does our soul undergo an evolutionary journey throughout eternity assisted by higher beings who encourage us to reflect on and assess the Earthly life we have just lived? These questions defy answers through an objective consideration of physical reality and lie beyond our Earthly human sense perception and experience. And yet the answers to all of these questions have been provided throughout this book in the observations the IANDS authors have brought back with them from beyond the veil.

For centuries, scientific materialism and reductionism have postulated that only physical matter exists and that a separate consciousness cannot subsist outside the human body. It is claimed that consciousness exclusively depends on the functioning human brain. Although this view has long been widely held and shared by the scientific and medical communities, this consensus is now being challenged. Sir John Eccles maintains that "the human mystery is incredibly demeaned by scientific reductionism ... we have to recognize that we are spiritual beings with souls existing in a spiritual world as well as material beings with bodies and brains existing in the material world." There is now a slow but inexorable emerging recognition within the scientific and medical communities that the human soul or consciousness survives the death of our physical body. The human brain does not create consciousness; rather, such consciousness is eternal by nature. And that is precisely the conclusion unanimously reported by all of the IANDS authors studied. The so-called phenomenon of the near-death experience reveals that the soul or consciousness survives the death of our physical body. Science (particularly in the realm of subatomic quantum physics) and spirituality are increasingly walking hand-in-hand with each other. As one IANDS author observed, humanity is now on the cusp of greater understanding, knowledge and evolution than at any time in its history.

Why should we accept this conclusion? After all, some of the concepts referred to in the NDE accounts, such as linear time as we experience it on Earth not existing in the higher dimensions, appear beyond human comprehension and plausibility. Yet most IANDS NDE authors report that their out-of-body experience had a deeply profound, tangible and enduring life-changing effect upon them. Their lives were never the same after their experience. They acquired new insights and knowledge into how we are supposed to live our Earthly lives and interact with others and what our Earthly mission and purpose are. They no longer fear death of the physical body and their faith in an afterlife (if they previously held any) was replaced by certain knowledge thereof. Our Earthly existence is but a dream; the Higher Spiritual Realms are the Ultimate Reality.

What is there to be learned from the messages from beyond the veil? We may summarize as follows:

- God/Source is the energy of unconditional love which permeates and connects all things and all of Creation; eternal, infinite, incorporeal, all-knowing and the Creator of All That Is. God is immanent in the sense of dwelling within each of us and omnipresent in the sense of being everywhere and in all things at the same time.

- Heaven (consisting of various levels) is part of the Ultimate Reality and is described by many IANDS authors as our real or true home. It can be considered as an emotional experience (of joy, bliss and euphoria), a spiritual frame of reference (in which negative energy or anything not of the Light is not permitted to enter) or a physical description by the soul's sense perception capacities (an intensely brilliant golden white Light which appears to have life and identity of its own as well as beautiful landscapes of vibrant and unearthly colors).

- All is an interconnected oneness. On Earth we live in a realm of apparent separation and separateness. We perceive our world as comprised of separate objects and people. Our Earthly reality is one of dualism in which the observer is separate or removed from what is being observed. But the concept of Universal non-dualism or oneness is beginning to emerge from recent research in the field of subatomic quantum mechanics. According to particle theory, the notion of separation and separateness is a complete illusion; every object is connected with every other object through energy and its vibrations. Each particle is connected to every other particle at the deepest foundational level of the Universe. In the spiritual realms, the observer and the observed cannot be separated as they are one.

- Our consciousness/soul/spirit is limitless and eternal energy, transcending a functioning human brain and existing on a pre- and post-human experience basis. As such, it survives the death of our body and brain. It comprises our true essence of who we truly are. Outside of our physical body, our soul is a receptor to elevated awareness and expanded consciousness; our bodies are merely temporary refuges enabling us to pursue our Earthly learning mission.

- Liberation of the soul through detachment elevates consciousness and spiritually awakens. The path to self-realization and enlightenment leads through separation from this world and all of its distractions and illusions. Detachment is a letting go of things which must be parted with in any event upon death of the physical body. It is an understanding of the relative unimportance and transient nature of power, fame and wealth as well as a cessation of desire and craving and suppression of the ego. Soul liberation also involves leaving behind fallacious human constructs such as the human misunderstanding of "death" and the linear nature of Time. We must also recognize the restrictive and debilitating nature of social, cultural and belief systems on our ability to perceive eternal Truths and Universal Laws as well as our natural but misplaced propensity to fear (which may be so consuming that we remain oblivious to the purpose and meaning of our Earthly life).

- The world of spirit is beautiful beyond description. There are countless universes, realms and dimensions, both seen and unseen, of vast complexity, some of which are connected to the Earthly plane. Negative energy, such as hatred, anger, aggression, greed, fear and judgment, has no place in the Higher Realms where only profound love, peace, understanding and acceptance may be encountered. Much of what we consider important in the Earthly realm is not considered as such within the Higher Realms where there is no longer any sense of self or ego and our Earthly identities have been left behind and been replaced by vibrations and light by which we as souls are recognized. What we experience in the spiritual realms is much more real than anything we have ever felt on Earth. The Earthly notion that only that which is physical or material and visible to the eye is real is a fallacy and illusion. The soul is much less limited and restricted in the spiritual realms than it is in the physical realm in not being bound by temporal-spatial constraints. Linear Time and Space as they are conceptually understood and experienced on Earth do not exist in the Higher Realms.

- While human knowledge and understanding of the seen physical realm we call Earth have been accumulating for millennia, we are now only on the threshold of a greater and more profound understanding of the unseen spiritual realms. Universal or Divine understanding is not the same as human understanding; only the former can enlighten the soul. Understanding is perceiving the way things actually are as opposed to the way we perceive them with our limited Earthly experience and comprehension; observing each phenomenon in its true nature as it actually is, rather than through the prism of material illusion or through the cultural-religious filter of one's lifelong accumulated individual conditioning. Outside the physical body, the soul receives instantaneous knowledge and awareness of how the physical and spiritual worlds operate and interact with each other. This infused knowledge has always been known by the soul-consciousness but temporarily forgotten during its Earthly incarnation. Trust and faith and belief held in the Earthly realm are superseded in the higher realms with certainty and proof of such matters as the existence of God/Source, Heaven, Beings of Light (including guardian angels and spirit guides), our life's purpose on Earth and reincarnation of the soul. The soul no longer believes because it knows.

- Communication in the spiritual realms is instantaneous unspoken dialogue between the deepest core of soul-consciousnesses. It involves the transfer of thoughts, concepts, ideas, knowledge, events and images, accompanied by associated feelings and emotions. Concepts and Universal Laws which are exceedingly difficult to comprehend with our limited Earthly knowledge and experience are instantly understood with ease in the higher spiritual realms.

- Life is a precious gift and all of us have a reason for being here. There is meaning and a higher purpose in everything and there are no coincidences in life. Each of us has an individual Earthly mission to complete, however modest that may be in the vast scheme of things. We are here to live life to the full and to derive joy from our experiences and relationships on Earth. We are here to explore and to learn and to love and be loved; to develop loving and caring relationships and to love and serve God by assisting others materially and spiritually. We are here to expand within ourselves our capacity for unconditional love and to manifest it towards others without expecting any personal benefits in return. And to be selfless rather than selfish. The inevitable struggles and challenges we face here are intended to assist us in developing strength and beauty of character and spirit. This is part of the Divine plan.

- Prior to birth in the Earthly realm, the soul voluntarily chooses its Earthly incarnation and accepts certain tasks or mission to be completed during its Earthly lifetime in order to serve God and spiritually evolve. In consultation with Beings of Light, the soul chooses the family it will be born into, the location and circumstances of birth, the length of Earthly life and the life lessons to be mastered. This overarching life plan or soul agreement permits the soul to experience life and its lessons in whatever form it has chosen.

- Free Will is a precious gift bestowed upon us by God. Our particular life experiences are chosen by us, and God honors and respects all of the decisions and choices we make for our lives but we remain responsible for them at the soul level. God grants Free Will to us to allow us to find our way or to blunder through life by letting us make our own choices when we reach the proverbial fork in the road. The choices we make either help us to achieve our soul's lifetime mission or take us further away from it. Sometimes we must fall, acknowledge our mistakes and pick ourselves up again for our souls to learn and grow. Free Will is vital to succeeding in our Earthly life's mission and in facilitating our ascendance into the higher spiritual realms. Our Earthly purpose is to grow towards the Divine, and for those who actively pursue and live by the positive energy of the Universe, there is great reward.

- We are to be compassionate towards, accepting of, and gentle with, ourself. We must not disrespect or judge ourselves or be too self-critical and overcome with guilt; otherwise, we cannot live our life to the full and it will be difficult for us to perceive the good and God in others.

- We awaken to the meaning and joy of our Earthly life through mindfulness. All things must pass. Since we cannot undo our past and have only tenuous control over the future, our exclusive focus must be an awareness of the present moment – the Eternal Now. We must rejoice in its preciousness as it will never come again. Maintaining a focused awareness of what one is doing, thinking and feeling in each moment, unencumbered by reflections of past regrets and anxieties concerning the future, assists us in performing our daily tasks wholeheartedly rather than superficially.

- All life is precious, beautiful and sacred. Elevated consciousness perceives God/The Creator/Source not only in other human beings but in all sentient beings as well as Nature itself. All life and the phenomena of Nature are imbued with spirit and consciousness. All physical and spiritual life and existence are interdependent and connected. God is in Nature (or Mother Earth/Gaia) as Creator and benevolent provider to all sentient beings. Reverence for God and Nature must extend to love and respect for the flora and fauna of this our most beautiful planet as well as gratitude for Earth's abundant blessings. Humanity's role is to be Nature's guardian or steward. Earth is our mother, a living organism from which humanity has much to learn. The Universal Laws require us to live in harmony with and respect Nature and not to take therefrom more than our needs require and what can sustainably be produced.

- What we sow is what we reap; all that we send forth into the Universe is sooner or later returned to us. Like understands and attracts like; what we think and speak about and do draws or manifests similar energy in kind to us. What our soul's energy emits draws similar energy back to us, positive or negative. This is how we create our own personal reality on Earth. These are respectively the Universal Laws of Cause and Effect and Attraction.

- The Universe and everything in it are energy which cannot be created or destroyed and which has always been, and always will be, moving in and through different forms and ever in transition. This is a Universal Law. God/Source is universal energy flowing through everything – humans, animals, plants, trees etc. – and making everything one. Everything is created from the same subatomic particles connected to Source energy. Our souls are the energy that is one with that of God/Source. Upon the death of our body, energy changes form and our soul-consciousness experiences higher vibrations. Everything exists in a continual balance between positive and negative energy. Each soul manifests positive and negative energy which finds its own equilibrium in the sense that positive energy attracts positive energy and negative energy attracts negative energy. Powerful positive energies include unconditional love, compassion, kindness, gratitude, acceptance, forgiveness and joy. Negative energy – such as fear, hatred, aggression, greed, selfishness, guilt and being judgmental – is not of God and does not exist in the Higher Realms. The manifestation of negative thoughts and deeds alters our soul's energy flow and triggers the Universal Law of Attraction whereby this negativity will surely be returned to us by the Universe.

- Our physical body – a temple of the Divine spark that dwells in each of us – is a perishable, temporary Earthly vessel or receptacle for our soul-consciousness or life-force which is eternal. Our body enables our soul-consciousness to experience Earthly life and to learn and grow therefrom. What humans refer to as death is the separation of the soul-consciousness from the physical body; a shedding of our physical existence and a transition of our soul-consciousness to a spiritually-based experiential existence in which our energy assumes a new form. Our re-birth into the spiritual realms transitions our soul to heightened and more acute thought, perception, awareness and consciousness. The death of our body is leaving behind our temporary home and returning to our real or true home. It is a natural continuation of an eternal process of our spiritual evolution towards God/Source.

- Between physical incarnations, the soul-consciousness undergoes a "life-review" in which the soul is shown a replay of the life just lived and invited to reflect on what it learned from its life experiences and interactions, and whether unconditional love and selfless caring for others were understood and practiced. The soul feels respectively the happiness, joy, pain, anger and hurt of those whom the soul was kind and insensitive to. The life-review is empathy personified; being in the shoes of others and feeling the effects of the soul's acts and omissions on others with whom it interacted. The outcome of the process is not judgmental but rather educational in nature; one's conduct is not so much wrong or mistaken but rather not helpful to the soul's evolutionary development. The soul discovers that what we consider important in the Earthly plane means little in the Higher Realms but what we consider insignificant on Earth is often most profound and meaningful. And the choices we make for our lives and our thoughts, words, deeds and omissions are more powerful and impactful than we can ever imagine and have enduring and unforeseen consequences. The soul's self-reflection on what it thought, spoke, did and did not do is an important step in progressing the soul's eternal evolutionary journey.

To sum up, Love is the most powerful force in existence and practicing unconditional love towards all beings and rendering small kindnesses thereto are therefore never misplaced. We should love all and injure none, while trying to make a difference by giving to life more than we receive from it. For those who have had a near-death experience, it is hoped that this book will provide validation and corroboration for what you experienced and observed. For those who are terminally ill or who fear the eventual demise of their physical body or for those who are grieving the loss of a loved one, it is hoped that this book will provide a measure of comfort, peace, solace and assurance that our souls are eternal and that a beautiful afterlife awaits us in the Higher Realms (our true home). For those who feel lost and confused, that we are never truly alone and that Higher Beings are constantly watching over us and assisting us if we permit them through the exercise of our proper intention and free will. For those who are experiencing difficulty discerning meaning or purpose in their life, we have been told that each of us has come to Earth to fulfil a particular assignment or mission in order to progress our soul's evolutionary journey towards communion with the Source. In order to recall what that mission is, we must penetrate through mindfulness and meditation the inner depths of our being to discover who we truly are and try to live more in alignment with the Light and positive energy. Separateness or duality is an Earthly illusion, for all of us and all of Creation are an interconnected energetic wholeness and oneness, like spokes radiating from the center of a wheel.

Author Biography

Douglas Hodgson is a dual citizen of Canada and Australia and a retired lawyer and Dean and Professor of Law residing in Perth, Western Australia. He undertook postgraduate legal study at the University of London before embarking on a 35-year career in higher education in Canada, Australia and New Zealand as a teacher, researcher, scholar, author, human rights advocate and university administrator. His areas of expertise include Public International Law, International Human Rights Law, International Humanitarian Law, Civil Law and Causation Law. Professor Hodgson has authored and published 30 peer-reviewed law journal articles and five books:

The Human Right to Education
(Dartmouth, Aldershot, Hampshire, England, 1998)
ISBN: 1-85521-909-3

Individual Duty within a Human Rights Discourse
(Ashgate, Aldershot, Hampshire, England, 2003)
ISBN: 0-7546-2361-0

The Law of Intervening Causation
(Ashgate, Aldershot, Hampshire, England, 2008)
ISBN: 978-0-7546-7366-8

International Human Rights and Justice
(Nova Science Publishers, Inc., New York, NY, USA, 2016)
(Editor)
ISBN: 978-1-63484-709-4

Transcendental Spirituality, Wisdom and Virtue: The Divine Virtues and Treasures of the Heart
(John Hunt Publishing, Winchester, Hampshire, England, 2023)
ISBN: 978-1-80341-143-9

Professor Hodgson's professional networks included the Australian Academy of Law, the Council of Australian Law Deans, the Global Law Deans' Forum and the Australian Research Council. He also served as an advisor to the Australian Red Cross, editor of several law journals and as a member of various university human research ethics committees. He is a regular attender and alumnus of the Oxford Round Table where he has delivered addresses on the concept of an international rule of law, the protection of children's international human rights and the challenges of religious fundamentalism in the public school system from a human rights perspective.

As a complement to his work on religious discrimination issues in the educational field, he developed a keen interest in studying and comparing the scriptures of the world's faiths and distilling therefrom common and unifying spiritual principles upon which these great and diverse religions are based, ultimately inspiring him to write *Transcendental Spirituality, Wisdom and Virtue: The Divine Virtues and Treasures of the Heart.*

His interest in transcendental spirituality has strengthened and expanded in his retirement years to include the so-called "near-death experience" and what humanity can learn from those who have returned from beyond the veil and recounted their experiences and observations. This has led to the writing of *Spiritual Revelations from Beyond the Veil: What Humanity Can Learn from the Near-Death Experience* in which these observations and insights have been collated, analyzed and commented upon.

Sources

IANDS, International Association for Near-Death Studies, Inc.
https://iands.org/ndes/nde-stories.html (NDE Accounts)

Eternea, The Convergence of Science and Spirituality for
Personal and Global Transformation
http:www.eternea.org

Recommended Reading

Raymond A. Moody Jr., MD *Life After Life* (HarperOne, New
York, NY, USA 10007, 2015)

Eben Alexander, MD *Proof of Heaven: A Neurosurgeon's Journey
into the Afterlife* (Pan Macmillan Australia Pty Ltd, Sydney,
NSW, Australia, 2012)

O-BOOKS

SPIRITUALITY

O is a symbol of the world, of oneness and unity; this eye represents knowledge and insight. We publish titles on general spirituality and living a spiritual life. We aim to inform and help you on your own journey in this life.
If you have enjoyed this book, why not tell other readers by posting a review on your preferred book site?

Recent bestsellers from O-Books are:

Heart of Tantric Sex
Diana Richardson
Revealing Eastern secrets of deep love and intimacy to Western couples.
Paperback: 978-1-90381-637-0 ebook: 978-1-84694-637-0

Crystal Prescriptions
The A-Z guide to over 1,200 symptoms and their healing crystals
Judy Hall
The first in the popular series of eight books, this handy little guide is packed as tight as a pill-bottle with crystal remedies for ailments.
Paperback: 978-1-90504-740-6 ebook: 978-1-84694-629-5

Take Me To Truth
Undoing the Ego
Nouk Sanchez, Tomas Vieira
The best-selling step-by-step book on shedding the Ego, using the teachings of *A Course In Miracles*.
Paperback: 978-1-84694-050-7 ebook: 978-1-84694-654-7

The 7 Myths about Love...Actually!
The Journey from your HEAD to the HEART of your SOUL
Mike George
Smashes all the myths about LOVE.
Paperback: 978-1-84694-288-4 ebook: 978-1-84694-682-0

The Holy Spirit's Interpretation of the New Testament
A Course in Understanding and Acceptance
Regina Dawn Akers
Following on from the strength of *A Course In Miracles*, NTI teaches us how to experience the love and oneness of God.
Paperback: 978-1-84694-085-9 ebook: 978-1-78099-083-5

The Message of A Course In Miracles
A translation of the Text in plain language
Elizabeth A. Cronkhite
A translation of *A Course In Miracles* into plain, everyday language for anyone seeking inner peace. The companion volume, *Practicing A Course In Miracles*, offers practical lessons and mentoring.
Paperback: 978-1-84694-319-5 ebook: 978-1-84694-642-4

Your Simple Path
Find Happiness in every step
Ian Tucker
A guide to helping us reconnect with what is really important in
our lives.
Paperback: 978-1-78279-349-6 ebook: 978-1-78279-348-9

365 Days of Wisdom
Daily Messages To Inspire You Through The Year
Dadi Janki
Daily messages which cool the mind, warm the heart and guide
you along your journey.
Paperback: 978-1-84694-863-3 ebook: 978-1-84694-864-0

Body of Wisdom
Women's Spiritual Power and How it Serves
Hilary Hart
Bringing together the dreams and experiences of women across
the world with today's most visionary spiritual teachers.
Paperback: 978-1-78099-696-7 ebook: 978-1-78099-695-0

Dying to Be Free
From Enforced Secrecy to Near Death to True Transformation
Hannah Robinson
After an unexpected accident and near-death experience, Hannah
Robinson found herself radically transforming her life, while a
remarkable new insight altered her relationship with her father, a
practising Catholic priest.
Paperback: 978-1-78535-254-6 ebook: 978-1-78535-255-3

The Ecology of the Soul
A Manual of Peace, Power and Personal Growth for Real People
in the Real World
Aidan Walker
Balance your own inner Ecology of the Soul to regain your
natural state of peace, power and wellbeing.
Paperback: 978-1-78279-850-7 ebook: 978-1-78279-849-1

Not I, Not other than I
The Life and Teachings of Russel Williams
Steve Taylor, Russel Williams
The miraculous life and inspiring teachings of one of the World's
greatest living Sages.
Paperback: 978-1-78279-729-6 ebook: 978-1-78279-728-9

On the Other Side of Love
A woman's unconventional journey towards wisdom
Muriel Maufroy
When life has lost all meaning, what do you do?
Paperback: 978-1-78535-281-2 ebook: 978-1-78535-282-9

Practicing A Course In Miracles
A translation of the Workbook in plain language, with
mentor's notes
Elizabeth A. Cronkhite
The practical second and third volumes of The Plain-Language
A Course In Miracles.
Paperback: 978-1-84694-403-1 ebook: 978-1-78099-072-9

Quantum Bliss
The Quantum Mechanics of Happiness, Abundance, and Health
George S. Mentz
Quantum Bliss is the breakthrough summary of success and
spirituality secrets that customers have been waiting for.
Paperback: 978-1-78535-203-4 ebook: 978-1-78535-204-1

The Upside Down Mountain
Mags MacKean
A must-read for anyone weary of chasing success and happiness
– one woman's inspirational journey swapping the uphill slog for
the downhill slope.
Paperback: 978-1-78535-171-6 ebook: 978-1-78535-172-3

Your Personal Tuning Fork
The Endocrine System
Deborah Bates
Discover your body's health secret, the endocrine system, and
'twang' your way to sustainable health!
Paperback: 978-1-84694-503-8 ebook: 978-1-78099-697-4

Readers of ebooks can buy or view any of these bestsellers by
clicking on the live link in the title. Most titles are published
in paperback and as an ebook. Paperbacks are available in
traditional bookshops. Both print and ebook formats are
available online.
Find more titles and sign up to our readers' newsletter at
http://www.johnhuntpublishing.com/mind-body-spirit
Follow us on Facebook at https://www.facebook.com/OBooks/
and Twitter at https://twitter.com/obooks